Also of interest

Platte River Road Narratives

A Descriptive Bibliography of All Known Eyewitness Accounts of Travel over the Great Central Route to Oregon, California, Utah, Colorado, Montana, and Other Western States and Territories, 1812–66

MERRILL J. MATTES

Foreword by James A. Michener

This massive annotated bibliography fills a conspicuous gap in historical literature by cataloging all known substantive central overland accounts written during the half-century prior to the advent of the transcontinental railroad. *Platte River Road Narratives* contains over two thousand entries extracted from diaries, journals, recollections, and letters.

"Nothing can compare with this work in scale, scope, and sophistication. It will be the ultimate Michelin Guide for overland trails material. No research, university, college, western, or genealogical library could do without it. Collectors of western Americana will find it indispensable."— Martin Ridge, co-editor of *America's Frontier Story: A Documentary History of Westward Expansion.*

Images of America

Images of America

Travelers from Abroad in the New World

Robert B. Downs

University of Illinois Press
URBANA AND CHICAGO

Images of America

© 1987 by the Board of Trustees of the University of Illinois
Manufactured in the United States of America
C 5 4 3 2 1

Pages 212–15 from *Farewell to America* by Henry W.
Nevinson (B. W. Huebach, 1922). Reprinted by
permission of Viking, Penguin, Inc.

This book is printed on acid-free paper.

Library of Congress Cataloging-in-Publication Data

Images of America.

  Bibliography: p.
  Includes index.
  1. United States—Description and travel.
2. Travelers—United States—History—Sources.
I. Downs, Robert Bingham, 1903– .
E161.5.I53 1987 917.3′04 86-25014
ISBN 0-252-01399-9 (alk. paper)

Dedicated to the best, brightest, and youngest generation of American travelers: William, Alison, Terence, Jr., and Mary Elizabeth, who will create their own images.

Contents

Acknowledgment

Indebtedness should be expressed to a number of friends and family who helped to bring the present work to completion: Sheryl Gocking for typing the manuscript, Deloris Holiman for proofreading and general corrections, Jane Bliss Downs for proofreading and overall criticism, and John T. Flanagan for recommendations on content. Because of my own temporary physical disability, source materials for research were assembled for me from the University of Illinois Library by Rolland Stevens, Charles Shattuck, Phillips Garman, Donald Krummel, Kenneth Ekstrom, William Huff, and Terry Weech. The index was compiled by Clara D. Keller. Special appreciation is owed to the editor of this book, Mary L. Giles.

Introduction

Background

Relatively few prerevolutionary visitors to America came as casual tourists whose aim was to see and then to return home to write accounts of their impressions. Those who made the long transatlantic voyage, for a variety of reasons, usually expected to remain. They included colonists searching for a better life, some to unite with others of their religious faith and a certain number otherwise motivated. On the North American mainland, exploration and colonization were followed by settlement. There was little record during that early period of traveling beyond the limits of the outlying pasture lands and adjoining home sites.

The original motive for printing the reports of travelers seems to have been the promotion of land sales. Land speculators attempted to lure prospective buyers through exciting accounts of opportunities awaiting them in the new world.

Other incentives drawing travelers from abroad included simple curiosity to see new lands at first hand; literary ambitions (some travel books were best-sellers); and occasionally to test certain social, political, and religious theories. A perceptive explanation was offered by Edward Freeman in 1883 in his *Some Impressions of the United States:* "'What do you think of our country?' is the question traditionally put into the mouth of the American addressing his British visitor. And the British visitor in real life finds that he very often has to answer the same question or its equivalent . . . it is easy to see an intense desire on the part of the American host to know how everything about him looks in the eyes of the British guest." A young nation often censured and misunderstood is keenly sensitive to the opinion of other nations. Thus, even highly critical works, such as those by Dickens, Harriet Martineau, and Frances Trollope, were sharply resented but were widely read.

Bibliographic roundups of foreign travelers' accounts of their American experiences date back at least to the Civil War era. Perhaps the first was Henry T. Tuckerman's *America and Her Commentators, with a Critical Sketch of Travel in the United States,* issued by Charles Scribner in 1864. Tuckerman begins with Columbus and proceeds to analyze the accounts of British, French, Italian, Northern European, and American writers down to the mid-nineteenth century.

Also dealing with the beginning of American history are two Yale University Library exhibitions collectively titled "Image of America, 1494–1788," a catalog of which was published in the *Yale University Library Gazette* (October 1976) edited by Kenneth M. Neishem, recording 118 works on the discovery, exploration, and settlement of the Western Hemisphere until after the Revolution.

A comprehensive summary by Allan Nevins, *America through British Eyes,* published in 1948 by Holt, is more restricted geographically, but records more than 400 titles by 367 authors. Two similar works had appeared under Columbia University's auspices: Jane Louise Mesick's *The English Traveller in America, 1785–1835* (1922), and Max Berger's *The British Traveller in America, 1836–1860* (1941). Mesick lists and discusses 78 titles, to which Berger's "Critical Bibliography" adds well over 300 travel accounts, tourist and emigrant guidebooks, and biographical-historical-critical reviews.

Also broad in scope are Henry Steele Commager's *America in Perspective: The United States through Foreign Eyes* (Random House 1947), including selections from the accounts of 35 travelers representing almost as many nationalities; and *Abroad in America: Visitors to the New Nation, 1776–1911,* edited by Marc Pachter and Frances Wrin, and sponsored by the National Portrait Gallery, Smithsonian Institution, reviewing the careers and travel chronicles of 29 travelers from nearly as many countries.

A similar approach was made by Oscar Handlin in his *This*

Was America: True Accounts of People and Places, Manners and Customs, as Recorded by European Travelers to the Western Shore in the Eighteenth, Nineteenth, and Twentieth Centuries (Harvard University Press, 1949), reviewing some 40 works by different European observers.

A related work in the same field is John Graham Brooks's *As Others See Us,* published by Macmillan in 1908 and dedicated to the celebrated British political scientist Sir James Bryce. Although Brooks's primary attention is focused on the British, he also examines French and German points of view.

Travel accounts are adequately recognized by three different writers in the *Cambridge History of American Literature:* George Parker Winship's "Travellers and Explorers, 1583–1763"; "Travellers and Observers, 1766–1846," by Lane Cooper; and "Travellers and Explorers, 1846–1900," by Frederick S. Dellenbaugh. The last work also contains detailed bibliographic references.

It is difficult to estimate the total number of accounts by foreign travelers of their American observations. For the period 1763–1846 alone, one bibliographer recorded 413 titles of works bearing upon the single state of Illinois.

A major resource also is Edward G. Cox's *A Reference Guide to the Literature of Travel* (University of Washington, 1935–49) The second of his three volumes is devoted to "The New World" and is particularly complete for the colonial period and up to about 1800.

The great influx of travelers, who came for periods of a few months to several years, did not come until the late eighteenth and the nineteenth century. The background comments that follow relate primarily to that exciting era, as visitors from England, Germany, France, Italy, and elsewhere reacted to what they observed from the Atlantic to the Pacific in America. The concentration is on the postrevolutionary United States, although accounts of travel in Canada, Mexico, and South America are also numerous and often make fascinating reading.

Who Were the Travelers?

Foreign visitors to America in the postrevolutionary period and on into the twentieth century were of infinite variety. In his *The British Traveller in America,* Max Berger listed authors, journalists, lecturers, scientists, businessmen, clergymen, soldiers, politicians, artists, promoters, actors, songwriters, and sportsmen, and even these did not exhaust the "Kaleidoscopic array." Many came as prospective emigrants and, having failed to make a go of it, returned home disillusioned. Others came for reasons of health.

Travelers who were known to have specific missions included an advocate of phrenology, a promoter of Illinois farm lands, a famous geologist, Lyell, to carry on research, religious leaders to attend denominational conventions, buffalo hunters, artists to paint the American landscape, government representatives, and military officials (who were usually stationed in Canada, but who spent their vacations in the United States). All were probably outnumbered by mere tourists, curious to gather their own impressions of the new lands and encouraged by the cheapness of American travel—about one-half as expensive as in Britain.

In the mid-nineteenth century, a great wave of emigration followed the Irish Famine and the European revolutions of 1848 and the discovery of gold in California.

The published accounts naturally reflected their authors' prime concerns, such as George Lewis on American churches, Hugh Seymour Tremenheere on schools, Horton Rhys on the theater, George Berkeley on hunting, Lauchlan Mackinnon on naval matters, Frederick J. Jobson on Methodism, Marianne Finch on feminism, Fanny Kemble on slavery, Richard Francis Burton on the Mormons, George Oliver on western agriculture, George Frederick Ruxton on the Indians and fur-trappers of the Rockies, Luther Sage Kelly on the roaring mining camps of California, and Robertson, Hancock, and Prentice on commercial enterprises.

Rapid improvements in transportation also accounted for the horde of visitors who came to America after 1848. Transatlantic travel on several lines was marked by a new era of steam, speed, and comfort. Slow-moving sailing packets were being replaced by steamers. In the more remote regions of the South and West, the stage coach was still the mainstay of transportation, but railroads were displacing both stages and canals in the East. By 1860, the country's railroad mileage had grown to 30,640. Transport by river steamer was popular on western rivers.

Nearly all authors of travel accounts were members of the aristocracy or the middle class; the poor and uneducated were primarily inarticulate. The motives for writing about travels were almost as diverse as the travelers themselves. Financial rewards could be substantial, because there was a tremendous market for books on America. Often the travelers came with particular biases or points of view that they tried to validate with their own observations. The consequences are well summed up by Max Berger: "Actually, far from being models of impartiality and scientific objectivity, the travel accounts reflect the interests, the biases, the preconceptions, and the viewpoints of their authors. The traveller saw new scenes, but through his old spectacles. As a result, all too often it came about that the Tory found American conditions intolerable; the Whig reported them with sympathy; and the Radical used them as ammunition for attacks upon conditions at home."

Travel Routes

Early travelers from abroad usually landed in New York or Boston, although some entered by way of Savannah, Newport News, or New Orleans. If the point of origin was New York, it was a frequent practice to go on to Albany and Buffalo. A visit to Niagara Falls was mandatory, and many visitors included Canada in their itinerary. Other popular destinations were Philadelphia and especially Washington. Those curious about the South, particularly persons who wanted to investigate slavery at first hand, went on to Richmond, Charleston, and Savannah, and perhaps by stage and boat to New Orleans. There, hardy travelers favored voyages up the Mississippi to the mouth of the Ohio.

Explorers of the West had several routes open to them. By the end of the Revolution, Virginia and Pennsylvania had well-defined roads to the Ohio, and early in the nineteenth century

Maryland built a national thoroughfare, the Cumberland Road, from Cumberland to Wheeling, West Virginia, on the Ohio. The Erie and Pennsylvania Canals also expedited western travel until the coming of railroads. These were some of the early attempts to penetrate beyond the Allegheny ridge, which as James Hall wrote, "presented a formidable barrier, and those who crossed it found themselves in a new world where they must defend themselves or perish. It was the Rubicon of the adventurous traveler."

The continual expansion of stage, steamer, and rail lines by 1860 made it almost commonplace for travelers to cross the continent. Most travelers were less venturesome, however, and left the Plains and California out of their American itinerary.

Manners and Customs

A common feature of foreign travelers' accounts of their experiences in the New World was attempts to analyze the character of Americans. How did the manners and customs that they encountered differ significantly from those back home?

The strongest single impression, as recorded by the visitors, was the Americans' aggressive spirit of independence and equality. In travel, hotel accommodations, and political affairs, there were no distinctions of rank or class. This attitude derived in good part because extremes of wealth and poverty were generally lacking. One result was the great difficulty in finding domestic help, associated by Americans with slavery. Servants could only be attracted by high wages and special treatment. Servants had to be recruited, therefore, primarily among free blacks and Irish emigrants. Some commentators were so irked by the situation that they concluded slavery was the best solution to the servant problem.

Related to the servant problem was the general American aversion to menial labor, often reported by the travelers. This type of labor was left to free blacks, Irish emigrants, and in California to Chinese coolies. That this spirit has not disappeared in modern America is demonstrated by the dependence on Mexicans and other immigrants for stoop labor in harvesting crops in the South, Southwest, and California.

Despite the insistence on equality, visitors observed social differences in American society based on such factors as education, income, and sometimes family pride. Associated with the feeling of some persons that they were more equal than others was the Americans' love for titles, explaining the prevalence of such appelations as captain, colonel, general, or judge, often with slight basis in fact.

Perhaps related was the American's ingrained habit of bragging. Americans was convinced that their country was the greatest in the world, their government the most democratic, their laws the most enlightened, and their institutions the most praiseworthy. For the same reasons, they were intolerant of any criticism from foreigners, denouncing as slander any written or spoken disparagement of their country.

But there were, of course, justifications for criticism. One of the most disgusting American habits in the eyes of visitors was the widespread use of chewing tobacco, accompanied by constant spitting. Such observers as Harriet Martineau noted that the tobacco-chewers fouled the floors of boarding houses, the decks of steamboats, the carpets of the Capitol in Washington, theaters, and even the pews of churches. Spittoons were everywhere, and some of the culprits developed remarkable accuracy in hitting them from several feet away.

Another American foible that drew frequent critical comments was constant drinking. Actual drunkenness was uncommon, but apparently nothing could be done without a drink. Liquor was consumed by stage passengers at every stop, and bars were the universal meeting places. The variety of alcoholic beverages available was noteworthy: rum, rye, and corn whiskey, peach and apple brandy, hard cider, mint juleps—all plentiful, cheap, and of good quality. Even children were allowed to indulge.

Food was plentiful in homes and inns, and there was substantial variety: veal cutlets, beefsteaks, chicken, ham, eggs, cheese, and sweets. Diets were likely to be heavy, with much consumption of animal food. The American fondness for greasy food was often criticized, as were table manners that were marked by wolfing food and crude eating manners such as reaching across the table for food and using one's own knife and fork to carry something to one's plate.

Judging by newspaper stories and their own observations, visitors concluded that Americans were a lawless people. Laws were plentiful, but well-organized police forces were not available to enforce them, even in large cities like New York. Dueling was common, perhaps a survival of frontier traditions, and family feuds were characteristic in some regions of the South. Cases of mob violence, usually directed at abolitionists and Negroes, were more typical of the South, although not rare in the North and West. Widespread lawlessness and crime were blamed by some critics on the evil influence of slavery or on heavy drinking, and on a general disregard for human life.

Another charge brought against Americans by visitors was that they were too inquisitive, annoying the traveler by asking too many questions of a personal nature. At the same time, the natives were as willing to answer questions as to ask them. Charles Dickens, for example, complained about the lack of privacy, being too much lionized, and being asked impertinent questions.

Women and Family

The importance of women in a country being newly settled was widely recognized. American men treated them with quixotic chivalry, and women traveled everywhere unchaperoned and unmolested. A high state of morality prevailed. Young women were generally considered beautiful, but they aged rapidly, a circumstance blamed on climate, diet, and lack of exercise. Bad teeth were often a disfiguring feature. Women's dress, especially in the cities, was harmful to their health and vigor because of the light and flimsy attire fashionable for winter wear. Female education generally ceased at twelve or fourteen, although a few young women were given a smattering of French and some instruction in music and dance. Nevertheless, American women were active readers, chiefly of novels.

Marriage was practically the only career open to women in the nineteenth century, although a few were teachers, dressmakers, and factory workers. Very early marriages, sometimes by age twelve, were the rule, and each union produced an average of six children. It was not uncommon for a woman to have a family by the time she was eighteen. Indigent older people were cared for in their children's homes. Log cabins, typical residences in the colonial and early statehood periods, were gradually replaced by wooden frame houses and later by brick or stone buildings. Food was plentiful, although often poorly prepared because of lack of training on the part of the women. Larger communities yielded a variety of social life and amusements.

Agriculture and Industry

America was, of course, a predominantly agricultural society until the twentieth century. Manufacturing industries were slow to develop, and imports supplied most demands for factory-made products. Land was plentiful and cheap. Farmers were held in high esteem and played an important part in public life.

A typical farm, perhaps slightly idealized, was described by Thomas Cooper on the basis of one that he visited in Pennsylvania in 1795: In addition to 300 acres and house and barns, it included a fish pond, a distillery, an icehouse, a smokery for hams and bacon, a saw mill, and a grist mill. Self-reliance was a key element for a comfortable and satisfying life.

The southern states' agriculture emphasized two money crops, tobacco and cotton. Travelers observed that the system of growing tobacco without rotation of crops soon exhausted the soil. Cotton grew well in all the southern states and occupied the slaves and most other people several months of the year. Louisiana turned out to be an ideal state for the cultivation of sugar. Western lands were given over principally to wheat and corn and to pasturing sheep and cattle.

A number of observers commented on a peculiar feature of rural life in America: the fences with which farmers surrounded their lands. The fences took a variety of forms—long wooden bars, rails, stone walls (primarily in New England), and live hedge fences.

Before larger scale manufacturing, domestic manufacture went on in practically every American home and farm, as foreigners frequently noted. Saw mills and grist mills were available for the sawing of logs and grinding of wheat; wool and flax were spun or woven into coarse cloth. Isaac Weld reported that in Virginia, at the beginning of the nineteenth century, slaves were trained as tailors, shoemakers, carpenters, blacksmiths, wheelwrights, weavers, and tanners.

Manufacturing on a substantial scale began in New England because of favorable sites, a long coast line to facilitate the export of manufactured products, and a surplus of labor for factories. Cotton mills in particular proliferated, and a high percentage of the mill operatives were women. Later established were paper mills; factories for the production of sheet iron, steel, nails, anchors, and sailcloth for shipping; and boat and shoe factories.

Thomas Cooper, John Melish, Isaac Weld, and other foreign observers reported from New England that the Middle Atlantic states, especially Pennsylvania and New York, began to produce a variety of manufactured goods.

The first settlers were not interested in mining. Gradually, however, exploitation began on a fairly large scale of iron and copper mines in Virginia, gold mines in North Carolina and elsewhere, and coal, salt, iron, lead, and nitre deposits in western states.

Some discontent and dissatisfaction with labor conditions were mentioned by a few observers, chiefly on the basis of long hours of work rather than of wages. Labor unions were a later development.

Slavery

Pre-Civil War visitors from abroad viewed slavery as a direct contradiction of Americans' claims for democracy in government. A frequent inquiry was, "If you have a land of equality before the law, why do you continue slavery?" Some of the most perceptive comments came from de Tocqueville. If dark troubles were ahead of the Americans, he concluded, "They will be brought about by the presence of the black race on the soil of the United States. . . . The troubles will owe their origin not to equality, but to the inequality of conditions." Charles Dickens was even more outspoken in his condemnation of "All those owners, breeders, users, buyers, and sellers of slaves, who when they speak of freedom, mean the freedom to oppress their kind, and to be savage, merciless, and cruel."

In the same vein, foreign critics, as they surveyed the American scene, were most in despair about the South. At least thirty visitors whose published accounts have survived came primarily to study the institution of slavery and its social effects. They were almost universally charmed by the manners and hospitality of their southern hosts. At the same time, they saw the roots of industrial and political society under the American form of government being poisoned by slave labor, resulting in giving the whites contempt for honorable work and making the whole theory of political equality ridiculous.

No trip to America was considered complete without a personal investigation of the problem of slavery. Even though the visitor did not undertake an extended tour of the South, he or she nearly always managed a side-trip there. The abolition of slavery in the British colonies and the long-drawn-out abolitionist controversy in the United States kept the subject alive. Visitors made disparaging comments on living conditions in the South: ill-built houses going to ruin, broken-down fences, dilapidated railroads, impassable roads, and dirty inns, providing a sharp contrast to the energy, activity, and enterprise prevailing in the North. The cruel treatment of slaves was attested to by numerous commentators. On the other hand, apologists for slavery were not lacking, few favored outright abolition, and no ready answer to the problem was clear. Unless a workable solution could be found, however, pre-Civil War visitors saw slavery as the most momentous problem confronting the Union, and predicted that civil war was inevitable unless the matter was resolved. In 1857, four years before the outbreak of the Civil War, James Stirling foresaw secession as inevitable because of the uncompromising, violent mood of the South. A few years earlier, in 1851, J. F. W. Johnston noted the greater material strength of the South and was convinced that America would never accept dissolution of the Union.

Education and Literature

In America, foreign observers found the system of popular nonsectarian education as firmly established as democratic government itself. In every region of the country, popular education was viewed as fundamental, the foundation upon which American institutions rested. Some opposition was noted to free common school education among wealthy people, who preferred to send their children to private schools, but a great majority were willing to tax themselves in order to support public schools.

The quality of education varied naturally from community to community. The systems prevailing in the larger cities, such as New York, Philadelphia, and Boston, won highest praise from critics. The most inadequately supported schools and the highest rate of illiteracy were found in the South.

Conservatives who opposed the entire theory of popular secular education called secular schools not only nonreligious but also irreligious, urged both religious control and religious education to produce a moral population, objected to attention to the physical sciences as too materialistic, and insisted on the need for stricter discipline and obedience toward authority.

Keen interest in higher education was also apparent in some chronicles of travel. By 1850, there were 123 colleges in the United States, with 435 instructors and enrolling 10,000 students. Harvard, generally regarded as the leading American college, was the most frequently visited. In the South, the University of Virginia drew chief attention from travelers because of its association with Thomas Jefferson. A majority of the colleges struggled with poverty and inefficiency, unable to attract capable presidents and professors because of poor salaries.

A related subject was the state of literature in America. Foreign opinion was generally critical, exemplified by Sydney Smith's question, "Who reads an American book?" The inferior quality of literature was blamed on such factors as scanty libraries; the cost of publishing original works; the fact the nation's active talent was preoccupied with commercial, agricultural, or professional pursuits; and lack of government patronage.

Nevertheless, it was observed that many books were sold in the

United States. A majority of these were cheaper reprints of foreign books, chiefly English. Novels and poetry were most in demand. Walter Scott was immensely popular. Such standard works as Shakespeare and Milton were reprinted in great numbers. Washington Irving and James Fenimore Cooper were popular at home and abroad. Philadelphia possessed a number of good book shops and a multitude of publishing houses. In general, the public demand was for a great deal of trash—a demand promptly met by publishers and booksellers.

English authors, such as Charles Dickens, were bitterly critical of American publishers pirating their writings; books were reprinted almost as soon as they appeared in England, of course without any compensation for their writers.

Libraries and museums were other resources for popular education and recreation that strangers often visited, especially in the larger cities. Outstanding was Benjamin Franklin's Library Company of Philadelphia, which a traveler in 1810 reported owned 14,000 books. New York had many libraries; noteworthy was the New York Library founded before the Revolution, which was reported in 1806 to contain 10,000 volumes. The contents of the Library of Congress were destroyed by the British in the War of 1812, but by 1832 it had accumulated 20,000 books.

Religion

The most striking fact about religion in America, especially to English visitors, was the absence of an established church. The idea of making religious observance and support entirely voluntary with the individual was a revolutionary innovation for many commentators from abroad. The consequences were interpreted from quite contrary points of view. Orthodox Anglicans were convinced that American religious tolerance was actually indifference to religion. The clergy was poorly educated, dependent upon their congregations for extremely meager pay, and subject to arbitrary dismissals. Another criticism of voluntary religion was that it led to a proliferation of sects, some belonging to the "lunatic fringe," such as the Millerites and the Shakers. Church services, it was charged, were attended primarily by women and old people.

More liberal-minded travelers, however, saw matters differently and concluded that America was basically a very religious country. The supporting evidence was found in the large number of churches, liberal donations for religious purposes, crowded church services, the superiority of American church music over the English, the puritanical observance of the Sabbath, the introduction of the Sunday school, and the founding of the American Bible Society.

Unorthodox religious sects were a favorite theme for travelers from abroad. The Millerites, whose principal tenet was a belief that the world would come to an end on a certain day in 1843, converted thousands. One observer attended a Millerite convention at which more than 5,000 people were present. The Shakers were yet another sect, living together under a rule of strict celibacy in agricultural communities. Later, by the mid-nineteenth century, the Mormons became the great American religious curiosity because of their conflicts with the federal government, their spectacular migrations, and their doctrine of polygamy.

Meanwhile, more standard sects and denominations were spreading across the country, as noted by many foreign observers. The Methodists and Baptists were considered to be largest in number, Episcopalians the most fashionable, and Presbyterians the wealthiest and most intelligent. Unitarians were numerous in the Boston area. Depending upon the region of the country, substantial numbers of Congregationalists, Dutch Reformed, Quakers, and various minor sects were well represented. Some commentators viewed with alarm the proliferation of Protestant sects, opening the way, they believed, to Catholics becoming the dominant church in America, especially after the vast German and Irish migrations of the 1840s.

Religious revivals were a common feature of most denominations and filled the foreign observers with curiosity. The inspiration generally came from a powerful preacher or evangelist, the people assembled in great numbers, and the meetings continued for several days. A phenomenon of particular interest to the travelers was the camp meeting, where thousands of people assembled in a great open space, pitched their tents for a week's stay, and preaching and prayer went on among tremendous demonstrations of religious enthusiasm. Although attempts were made to restrain immoral behavior, such a charge was frequently made against these gatherings.

Indians

The list of books on American Indians is enormous, and foreign travelers contributed their share. The Indians naturally resented seeing their game destroyed by newcomers, their springs polluted by cattle, and themselves treated with brutality and contempt. The whites, on their part, regarded the Indian as a dangerous nuisance to be got rid of in any way possible. The Indians' hostility naturally added to the perils of cross-country and western travel. One American who viewed the Indian with sympathy during the early western days was George Catlin, famous for his paintings and books. The Mormons were also generous in dealing with the Indians, being fair to them and paying them. However fear of Indians deterred timid travelers from going very far west.

Government

The American political system was an aspect of American life of profound interest to many foreign observers. Those who arrived with prejudiced opinions, liberal or conservative, generally returned home with their views confirmed.

Washington, the nation's capital, was considered a must for visitors. Those who anticipated seeing another London or Paris were naturally disappointed, especially during the years when construction was in progress. The large, half-finished buildings, the desolate appearance of the Potomac flats, and the great distances between buildings left an impression of a raw, unfinished city. Both the city's location and planning were considered unfortunate.

The accessibility and democratic behavior of the president amazed visitors and drew favorable comments. Receptions in the White House for thousands of guests were a common occurrence, and the president was ready to shake innumerable hands and to greet the hordes of job seekers and mere tourists. As Berger noted, "Englishmen never quite got over the shock of seeing the Chief Citizen of the Republic walking, talking, eating, and praying like the average man in the street."

Nevertheless, foreigners were critical of the manner of selecting presidents. With such leaders as Clay, Webster, and Calhoun available, they could not understand the election of such mediocrities as Harrison, Fillmore, Pierce, and Buchanan. Tories were convinced that the masses of voters were too ignorant to make the best choices. As Alexander Mackay pointed out, the best nominee was "the one least objectionable to all."

Next to the president, Congress was Washington's most interesting feature. The lack of order and general decorum in the House repelled observers. Speeches were long, irrelevant, and, according to Captain Frederick Marryat, "full of eagles, star-spangled banners, sovereign people, clap-trap, flattery, and humbug." In contrast, the Senate was found to be a dignified orderly assemblage, its members as a whole high in intellectual ability. This condition was attributed to the indirect election of senators and to their greater age and experience.

Although state governments received little attention from foreign travelers, a much-criticized aspect was the popular election of judges. The low salaries paid judicial officers, it was charged, attracted only the least capable of the legal profession.

The popular interest in politics astonished the foreigner. Politics was a universal topic of conversation, there was endless electioneering, and campaigns were often marked by violent political discussions and partisanship. Universal suffrage and political democracy were blamed for the low intellectual level of electioneering and the reluctance of men of dignity, wealth, or social position to become candidates for public office. The large influx of Irish voters in the mid-nineteenth century was thought by some commentators to be a prime source of election frauds and political corruption. Even liberals were inclined to concede that the people's powers often exceeded their educational attainments. George Combe, writing in 1841, declared that "one ignorant man is not a fit ruler for a great nation, nor are ten million more fit for doing so."

Even so, social reformers from abroad, while recognizing faults and defects in a democratic nation, were predisposed to see many merits in the American system of government.

Conclusion

Foreign visitors found that travels in America had been one of the great experiences of their lives. Previous conceptions were modified to a limited extent in some instances, but the tendency was for old viewpoints to be strengthened. There was general agreement on the material wellbeing of the American people, although some maintained that the prevailing prosperity should be credited to vast natural resources rather than to democratic institutions.

In predicting the future of America, travelers in the first half of the nineteenth century saw slavery as a divisive force destroying the nation's unity. A growing divergence in sectional interests was also cited as causing disunity because of the tremendous size of the country and the lack of adequate transportation and communication facilities between the sections. Neither conservatives nor liberals could see any limit to America's material growth, a nation that—if it remained united—was destined to become one of the most powerful on earth.

The general influence of travelers and observers is difficult to estimate. The nation undoubtedly benefitted from their criticisms, whether favorable or unfavorable, which helped to induce needed reforms. Some element of truth was contained even in prejudiced accounts. The works of travel stimulated emigration. Today they increase our knowledge of American conditions and the development of American institutions at the time of their composition.

1. *Travels into North America*

The record of Peter Kalm's travels and observations is important because he was apparently the first trained naturalist to make a comprehensive and scientific study of the flora and fauna of the American colonies.

In accord with eighteenth-century custom, the title page of Kalm's account of his American travels summarized the contents: "*Travels into North America; Containing Its Natural History, and a Circumstantial Account of its Plantations and Agriculture in General, with the Civil, Ecclesiastical and Commercial State of the Country, the Manners of the Inhabitants, and Several Curious and Important Remarks on Various Subjects* by Peter Kalm, Professor of Natural History and Economy in the University of Åbo in Swedish Finland, and Member of the Swedish Royal Academy of Sciences."

The Swedish Academy of Sciences was founded in 1739 to stimulate and direct scientific study, especially in agriculture. The academy's leaders recognized the excellent opportunities for original, practical research in America. One of the era's main problems was to find ways in which to enlarge the number and varieties of useful plants and trees in Sweden by importing and planting foreign seeds. For that purpose it was decided to send a naturalist to America to obtain seeds hardy enough to thrive in Swedish soil. On the recommendation of the celebrated Swedish botanist Carl von Linne (Linnaeus), thirty-one-year-old Peter Kalm, professor of natural history and economy at Åbo and Linnaeus's former pupil, was appointed.

Kalm's journey was by way of England, where he had to wait

six months for a ship. He landed in Philadelphia in September 1748. During the next two and a half years, he wandered extensively through Pennsylvania, New York, New Jersey, and southern Canada. His primary mission was kept conscientiously in mind as he collected seeds and recorded information about plant and animal. But he appears to have been almost equally interested in a variety of other matters: bark boats, asbestos, toothache remedies, church services, building materials, hospitals, Indian dialects, longevity among settlers, tobacco pouches, oil wells, Jesuits, and refrigeration.

Kalm described literally hundreds of native plants and trees, assigned Latin names to them, analyzed their possible usefulness, and made comparisons with similar species back in Sweden when relevant. Also complete was his interest in animals, birds, fish, serpents, and insects. Among his favorite subjects were maple sugar, Indian corn, ticks, spruce beer, skunks, wild doves, grass-hoppers, prehistoric fossils, walnut trees, and rattlesnakes.

The Swedish Academy had asked Kalm to find a mulberry tree that would withstand the Swedish climate and that might serve to start silk manufacture in Sweden. He reported that the governor of Connecticut "brought up a great quantity of silk worms in his courtyard; and they succeeded so well and spun so much silk that they gave him a quantity sufficient for clothing himself and all his family." Kalm's attempts to obtain mulberry tree seed apparently did not succeed however, although he found several kinds of mulberries on which silk worms thrived.

One animal that Kalm was keenly anxious to see and about which he had heard rumors was the moose. He met with frustration, for no one he consulted had seen a moose, and he ended up doubting its existence.

Because Kalm was a well-trained scientist, most of his observations were accurate. Occasionally, however, he was a victim of the tall tales for which early Americans were famous. Although he expressed some skepticism, he believed a story he was told about male blacksnakes that, when disturbed during courtship, would pursue the intruder with amazing swiftness, trip him up by wrapping around his feet, and then bite him several times before retreating. Kalm related, and believed, an incident about a girl who sat down alone in the woods. Her proximity disturbed the amours of a blacksnake that became enraged, ran up her legs, and wrapped itself around her waist. Her black servant found her unconscious and had to cut the snake to pieces before he could remove it. The modest young lady was so mortified by the incident that she pined away and died within a year.

Both rattlesnakes and blacksnakes, according to what Kalm was told, have the power to fascinate birds and squirrels: The snake would lie under a tree, fix its eyes on a bird or squirrel above, and force it to come down and fall directly into its mouth. Equally farfetched was a story told Kalm by the famous naturalist John Bartram, who was reporting on the damage done to cattle by bears. When a bear catches a cow, Bartram claimed, it kills her by biting a hole into her hide and blowing into the hole with all its power until the cow swells excessively and dies.

Kalm came to America with letters of introduction to a number of prominent persons. He noted that "Mr. Benjamin Franklin, to whom Pennsylvania is indebted for its welfare and the learned world for many new discoveries in electricity, was the first who took notice of me and introduced me to many of his friends. He gave me all necessary instruction and showed me kindness on many occasions." Kalm was granted free use of the library Franklin had founded—still surviving today as the Library Company of Philadelphia.

Late in his career, Kalm became a Lutheran clergyman. In the various American communities visited, he usually included descriptions of the churches that he found. In Philadelphia, he mentions the principal features of the English Established, Swedish, German Lutheran, Old and New Presbyterian, Old German Reformed, New Reformed, Quaker, Anabaptist, Roman Catholic, and Moravian churches. A similar diversity was found in New York City with the addition of New and Old Dutch, French (for Protestant refugees), and a Jewish synagogue. Quaker meetings are described in detail, including Quaker peculiarities of speaking and preaching, manners, and clothes.

The question of longevity interested Kalm. He concluded that Americans age faster than Europeans. The Americans were "less hardy than Europeans in expeditions, sieges, and long sea voyages, and died in large numbers." The reasons were unclear, but Kalm was inclined to blame extremely changeable weather, recurring attacks of "fever and ague," impure water, excess consumption of fruit, and too much child bearing by the women, beginning at a tender age. Also, Europeans in North America, regardless of racial origin, always lost their teeth much sooner than did Europeans back home. The culprit here, according to Kalm, was the habit of drinking too much hot tea.

Kalm was critical of careless agricultural practices among American farmers. He observed that forests were cleared, leaving a rich soil that was used as long as it would bear any crops. No manure was used, and after the soil lost its fertility it became pasture for cattle. New fields would then be cleared. The long-time consequences of this practice were bad, leaving the soil depleted.

Kalm found three types of servants employed in the English-American colonies. Some were entirely free and served by the year. These servants received their food and wages but bought their own clothes. Indentured servants, people too poor to pay their passage from Europe, were a second type. By agreement with the ship's captain, they were sold for a period of years on their arrival, and their transportation paid by the new masters. Blacks, bought as slaves to serve as long as they lived unless freed by their owners, were a third type of servant.

The prevailing atmosphere of freedom in America impressed Kalm. It enabled many people of different languages and religions to live peacefully together. He noted that many Jews had settled in New York, received all sorts of privileges, had a synagogue, operated ships, and owned their houses, large country estates, and shops in town.

By Kalm's time, most Indians had sold their land along the coasts to Europeans. Consequently, one had to travel a considerable distance inland to find the first Indian habitations.

A hint of the revolution to come is found in remarks quoted by Kalm "that the English colonies in North America, in the space of thirty or forty years, would be able to form a state by themselves entirely independent of Old England." In fact, the colonies did become independent thirty years after this date. For the time being, however, the settlers needed protection against the French and the Indians.

The first detailed descriptions of Niagara Falls was written by Kalm in a letter to Benjamin Franklin, after a visit to that area in August 1750. His quaint sketch of the falls has been reproduced in published accounts of his travels.

The scope of Kalm's scientific interests is shown by his frequent comments on the weather and his careful meteorological records. From August 1748 to January 1750 he maintained a daily record of the temperature at different hours, the direction and strength of winds, and the state of the weather in general.

Kalm returned to Sweden in 1751, and the Swedish-language version of his travels was published at intervals between 1753 and 1761. An English translation appeared in 1770–71, and there were German, French, and Dutch translations during the same period.

2. Travels in North America in the Years 1780, 1781 and 1782

Many books on the United States were published in Europe shortly after the American Revolution. The Marquis de Chastellux's *Travels* remains one of the most readable and informative of this large crop. The author was one of three major generals who accompanied the French Expeditionary Force headed by General Rochambeau. He was present at Yorktown when Cornwallis surrendered and is shown in John Trumbull's painting of that historic event.

Chastellux's writings, however, are now chiefly of interest as an account of his travels, rather than as a war memoir. It is the story of journeys made between campaigns when he was free from the active duties of his command. The author's personal reactions, written by a man who wielded the pen as skillfully as he did the sword, shed much light on America of the period.

French aid to the American revolutionary cause was clandestine until 1778, when a formal alliance ended the period of secret aid. Chastellux sailed from Brest on May 1, 1780, on the flagship of Admiral de Ternay's fleet and reached Newport, Rhode Island, on July 11. He made his headquarters at Newport until the following summer, when he began to take an active part in the Allied campaign that culminated victoriously at Yorktown in October 1781.

One of the first towns Chastellux visited was Providence, Rhode Island, which he reported was "handsome" although having only one long street. It had a population of 2,500 and carried on an active shipping trade, aided by its favorable location. Merchant ships bought slaves in Guinea, transported them to the West Indies, and brought back woolens and other merchandise from England.

Meeting "a most beautiful girl," who served him at an inn near Providence, inspired Chastellux to comment that she had "like all American women, a very becoming, even serious bearing; she had no objection to being looked at, having her beauty commended, or even receiving a few caresses, provided it was without any appearance of familiarity or wantonness." In fact, Chastellux noted, "licentious manners are foreign in America."

The "vast country" of Vermont, Chastellux found, was being claimed by both Massachusetts and New York. It had no legally established government, but Ethan Allen, famous for the 1775 expedition against Ticonderoga that he undertook as leader of the "Green Mountain Boys," had taken charge. He had formed an assembly of representatives, was making land grants, and Vermont was being governed by its own laws.

When Chastellux arrived at Hartford in November 1780, all inns were full because deputies of Massachusetts, New Hampshire, Rhode Island, and Connecticut were holding one of their periodic meetings. Instead, he was provided lodging in the home of Colonel Jeremiah Wadsworth, who had been appointed by General George Washington to be Commissary General in charge of all purchases. Another interesting personality Chastellux met in Hartford was Jonathon Trumbull, governor of Connecticut for the previous fifteen years, whose whole career had been devoted to public affairs.

The overnight arrangements Chastellux made in Hartford were typical of the time. He discovered that when taverns were scarce or bad, or not conveniently located for travelers, it was the American custom to ask for hospitality in a private home, after which the host was paid as an ordinary innkeeper.

In the course of his far-flung travels, Chastellux naturally encountered a variety of accommodations in public inns and taverns, some excellent and others incredibly bad. He was critical of the food, commenting that "Americans heap indigestion one on another . . . to the poor, relaxed, and wearied stomach, they add Madeira, rum, French brandy, gin, or malt spirits, which complete the ruin of the nervous system."

As he rode along the Farmington River between Hartford and Farmington, Chastellux meditated on the Americans' "poverty of language" in naming natural objects; for example, the jay was simply a "blue bird," the cardinal a "red bird," every water bird a "duck," from the teal to the wood duck and large black duck. Likewise, the pine, the cypress, and firs were all "pine trees."

Chastellux was impressed by the high degree of cooperation among neighbors in a community. "In America," he remarked, "a man is never alone, never an isolated being." A new home was built in three weeks to a month. Neighbors showed their hospitality by pitching in to aid the newcomer. Their only compensation was sharing a cask of cider or a gallon of rum.

A night at Morehouse Tavern in Wingdale, New York, was shared with farmers and drovers taking 250 cattle from New Hampshire to the American army. They were "the strongest and most robust men I had seen in America," observed Chastellux. When he complimented them on their size and stature, he was told that the inhabitants of New Hampshire were strong and vigorous because the air there was excellent, the sole occupation was agriculture, and their blood was unmixed, all descended from English emigrants.

En route to join General Lafayette, Chastellux stopped to inspect West Point, the Hudson River setting of which made a tremendous impression on him. He had high praise for the commandant, General William Heath, and was impressed by the fortifications that had been installed. West Point had been established as a military post in 1778, only two years previously. Chastellux denounced Benedict Arnold, who was in command in 1780 and who had attempted to betray the post to the British.

Before reaching the New Jersey encampments of Lafayette and Washington, Chastellux passed a scenic wonder, Totowa Falls near Porterson, New Jersey, and described the sight in glowing terms.

The reunion with General Lafayette occurred on November 23, 1780. Chastellux was then introduced to General Washington and other American officers. During the days that followed Chastellux was able to spend a considerable amount of time in Washington's company, and his written tribute was memorable. There was praise for "the perfect harmony which reigns between the physical and moral qualities which compose his personality." Chastellux's characterization of Washington continued: "All love and admire him; all speak of him only in terms of affection and admiration. . . . His stature is noble and lofty. He is well built and exactly proportioned; his physiognomy mild and agreeable. . . . You have only the recollection of a fine face. He has neither a grave nor a familiar air, his brow is sometimes marked with thought, but never with worry; in inspiring respect, he inspires confidence, and his smile is always the smile of benevolence."

Continuing his travels late in November 1780, Chastellux stopped at Princeton, New Jersey, site of an important Revolutionary War battle. There he met John Witherspoon, president of the College of New Jersey (later Princeton University), the enrollment of which had declined to forty students because of the war. The library had gathered "a fairly extensive collection of books," but "most of these had been scattered" because of depredations by English soldiers.

In nearby Philadelphia, Chastellux met Martha Washington, who had just arrived from Virginia and was on her way to join her husband, "as she does at the end of every campaign." Chastellux described her as "about forty or forty-five, rather plump, but fresh and with an agreeable face." Also met there was Sarah Franklin (Mrs. Richard Bache), Benjamin Franklin's daughter. A visit was paid to the University of Pennsylvania library, where the principal exhibit appears to have been some astronomical equipment. During a later stay in the city, just before his return to France, the University conferred an honorary degree on Chastellux.

While in Philadelphia, Chastellux wanted to attend the churches and different places of worship. The first was a Quaker meeting, which he characterized as a "dreary and rustic assembly." By contrast, the Anglicans' ceremony was distinguished by excellent singing and organ music and handsome equipment. Concerning the many different sects, "some were strict and others lax, but all of them imperious and all of them self-opinionated."

Chastellux had been anxious to meet Thomas Paine, author of *Common Sense,* who then lived in Philadelphia, so an interview was arranged on December 14. Paine's apartment had "all the attributes of a man of letters; a room pretty much in disorder, dusty furniture, and a large table covered with books lying open and half-finished manuscripts." "Our conversation," reported Chastellux, "was agreeable and animated." Further, "the vivacity of his imagination and the independence of his character have rendered him better suited for reasoning on affairs, than for conducting them."

At the time of Chastellux's visit, Philadelphia had about forty thousand inhabitants. "The streets are wide and regular, and intersect each other at right angles." There were sidewalks for pedestrians, and the city was well equipped with hospitals, workhouses, and houses of correction.

After his stay in Philadelphia, Chastellux turned north again, through New Jersey to Albany, Schenectady, Saratoga, and other communities in New York and Massachusetts, and then back to Newport. Every day of his journey is described in detail. He arrived in Newport on January 9, 1781, "happy to have seen many interesting things and to have met with no accident."

Thus was concluded part one of Chastellux's travel account, but it by no means ended his American travels. The year 1781 was devoted to military operations as the war wound down. In April 1782, Chastellux began a journey into upper Virginia, the Appalachians, and to the Natural Bridge in Virginia, during the course of which he visited Williamsburg, Monticello, Petersburg, Richmond, and Westover. Most memorable was his stay with Thomas Jefferson at Monticello from April 13 to 16. Chastellux's admiration for Jefferson knew no bounds; he noted Jefferson's genius as a musician, draftsman, surveyor, astronomer, natural philosopher, jurist, and as a statesman who had taken a leading part in bringing about the Revolution. Jefferson was found to be a delightful conversationalist on classical literature, science, politics, the arts, and every other subject touched upon. He was thoroughly familiar with American natural history and was an expert meteorologist, Chastellux discovered.

After leaving Monticello, Chastellux went on to see the Natural Bridge, which he called a "magnificent spectacle, so awesome that some people can scarcely bear it." From there the route lay east by way of Petersburg, Richmond, and Westover to Williamsburg.

Chastellux offers extended observations on the institution of slavery as he observed it in Virginia. He saw the slaves as "ill lodged, ill clothed, and often overwhelmed with work," although many Virginians "treated their Negroes with great humanity." The number of blacks in the state, about two hundred thousand, equalled the white population. The ill effects of slavery were somewhat offset in Chastellux's view by enabling the Virginians to indulge in gracious living.

Chastellux gave high praise to the College of William and Mary, "a magnificent establishment which adorns Williamsburg and does honor to Virginia," noting particularly the "richness of the library" and the distinguished faculty. The college conferred a doctor of laws degree on Chastellux during the course of his stay.

Natural history drew Chastellux's attention as he traveled through the country, and he devotes several chapters to a discussion of such American birds as purple martins, hummingbirds, and starlings, and to the opossum.

Part 3 of Chastellux's travels shows him retracing earlier routes. In November and December 1782, he journeyed through New Hampshire, Massachusetts, and upper Pennsylvania. A highlight was a visit to Cambridge, "a little town inhabited only by students, professors, and the small number of servants and workmen whom they employ." Harvard University's activities were concentrated in one building that housed classrooms, a cabinet for astronomical, mathematical, and other scientific instruments, an "extensive" library, and large chapel.

On December 7, Chastellux stopped in Newburgh to bid farewell to General Washington, who was encamped in the American army's winter quarters. By December 12, he was back in Philadelphia. He returned to Paris in 1783.

Chastellux's knowledge of English made him an important intermediary in French dealings with the Americans. He was friendly, popular, and completely at ease in every kind of company—military conferences, fashionable drawingrooms, among literary people, and in roadside taverns, always a polished French aristocrat.

3. An Excursion to the United States of North America in the Summer of 1794

Henry Wansey's travels in America occurred eight years after the end of the American Revolution. He was an English clothier who retired in his early forties and thereafter devoted himself to travel, reading, and antiquarian research, writing on local history for the Society of Antiquaries and on wool growing for the Bath and West of England Agricultural Society.

Wansey landed in Boston early in May 1794, traveled as far south as Philadelphia, and returned to New York to set sail for England. In preparation for writing an account of his travels, he read extensively about the new world and kept detailed notes on his observations and impressions. His accounts of the three major American cities of the time, Boston, New York, and Philadelphia, are of special interest.

Boston, which forty years earlier had been America's largest city, was third at the time of Wansey's visit, with about 48,000 inhabitants. He was directed to the Bunch of Grapes hotel, recommended as the best in the city, where porter service was provided by free blacks. Wansey noted that "the negroes in this state are all free, and are a respectable body of people. They have a free-masons' club, into which they admit no white person." The hotel rooms were indifferently cleaned, and "we were much pestered with bugs." With two companions Wansey walked over to Cambridge, "where the principal university in the states is established—Harvard College, an excellent institution, well endowed, supports three hundred students and has two large handsome brick buildings." For public transportation, Boston had forty hackney coaches, "and for a quarter dollar you are carried to any part of the town." Religious observances had become more tolerant. It was no longer the custom "to put people in the stocks who were seen walking in the streets during Sunday service, and they no longer hang old women for witchcraft, as they did in the last century."

Wansey praised the spaciousness and convenient arrangement of the Boston harbor, where there were stores for "sugar and rice, bags of cotton and wool, lumber, iron bars, bags of nails, and, in short, every article of commerce." The harbor was full of shipping; in 1794, 464 vessels entered the port of Boston. In the suburb of Charleston, Wansey met Jedediah Morse, author of the *American Geographical Grammar,* "now universally taught in all the schools and seminaries throughout America." Printing shops in Boston produced three newspapers: *The Columbian Sentinel, The Mercury,* and *The Boston Gazette or Republican Journal.* The 1790 census reported that Boston's population was 38,038.

After leaving Boston on May 14, Wansey traveled on the New York Mail Coach. A breakfast stop was made at Weston, where passengers were served beefsteaks, coffee, bacon and eggs, veal cutlets, toast, and butter. The bill was high, perhaps, Wansey supposed, because George Washington had stopped at that inn. In Worcester, he "dined well on beef and veal, with plenty of greens, potatoes, and cucumbers . . . and as much good cyder as we could drink." Wansey paid a visit to Isaiah Thomas, the famous printer and bookseller, from whom he bought an almanac and newspapers. The women in the country towns had their hair plaited at full length down their backs like a queue, a "very unbecoming fashion" in Wansey's opinion.

Passing through New Haven, a stop was made at Yale College, an institution with two brick buildings that was in bad condition and "very dirty, particularly the library. The books were numerous, but very old and in bad condition." Equipment also included a good reflecting telescope and a variety of natural history objects. The Yale students had been sent home three months previously "on account of the epidemic of putrid fever, which then raged in the town."

An eight-hour voyage by boat from New Haven brought Wansey to New York City, which impressed him as "much more like a city than Boston." He admired the views of the New York harbor and shipping, Staten Island, Long Island, Brooklyn, and other sights, and in the evening went to the theater for a performance of Mrs. Cowley's play, *A Bold Stroke for a Husband.* At least a half-dozen newspapers were then published in the city: *Daily Advertiser, American Mercury, Daily Gazette, Diary, Evening Post,* and *Greenleaf's New York Journal.*

While in New York, Wansey met Joseph Priestley, the distinguished scientist who was newly arrived from England. Another celebrity was Vice President John Adams, traveling from Philadelphia to Boston, who was described as "a stout, hale, well-looking man of grave deportment, and very plain in dress and person."

On June 3, Wansey set off for Philadelphia, anxious to arrive there before Congress adjourned and anticipating "an opportunity of seeing that great man, General Washington, before he returns to Mount Vernon." En route, a stop was made at Princeton, where he found "a very handsome college, housed in a large brick building," and with an enrollment of ninety-five students. Many of the most eminent men in Congress, Wansey observed, had been educated there.

Congress was still in session when Wansey arrived in Philadelphia, and he proceeded to visit the House of Representatives. He commended the convenience of the chamber's arrangements and facilities provided for the members. Visitors were freely admitted, but demonstrations of any kind, pro or con, were strictly forbidden. The chief business of the House on the occasion of Wansey's visit was a discussion of seven resolutions introduced by James Madison to place restrictions and impose higher duties on the manufactures and navigation of foreign nations, primarily directed against Great Britain.

One of the most hopeful signs for the future of America Wansey quoted from a speech by Representative Lee of Virginia: "The most auspicious prognostication of an improving age, is *the great demand for cheap books,* and the universal establishment of book clubs, which has opened a new field for the cultivation of literature."

A few days later, Wansey was granted an interview with President Washington, who invited him to breakfast. He found "The President in his person, is tall and thin but erect; rather of an engaging than a dignified presence. He appears very thoughtful, is slow in delivering himself . . . the effect of much thinking and reflection." Wansey was almost extravagant in his praise of Washington's career "as a general in the field . . . head of a victorious army . . . as the president of the United States . . . or a private gentleman, cultivating his own farm."

Mrs. Washington herself made tea and coffee for her guests. She was described as "short in stature, rather robust; very plain in her dress, wearing a very plain cap, with her grey hair closely turned up under it."

In the evening, Wansey went to the new theater for a performance of Mrs. Inchbald's play, *Every One Has His Faults.* "It is an elegant and convenient theatre, as large as Covent Garden," he reported, and the cast was English, most of whom Wansey had seen in England.

The next day Wansey visited the Benjamin Franklin Library, "one of the handsomest buildings I have yet seen." The library contained a well-selected collection of twelve thousand books for the use of its subscribers and for other persons for a nominal sum. Later, Wansey saw the house where Franklin had lived and died, and met Franklin's daughter, Mrs. Bache, "a very handsome, pleasing woman," and his grandchildren.

The year before Wansey's visit to Philadelphia, the city had been devastated by a yellow fever epidemic, during the course of which 4,992 persons were known to have died. Wansey offers a graphic account of the horrors of the time—panic among the people, many attempting to flee the city, a shortage of doctors, nurses, and morticians, the contagious nature of the disease, a breakdown of business, and general disorder.

Late in his travels, Wansey inspected the land, then estimated at four thousand acres, on which the new capital city of Washington was to be built. The plans for what he referred to as "Federal City" had been designed by Washington himself, who had waited for a propitious time to initiate them. From Wansey's point of view, the location had many important advantages. The projected scheme provided for a national university, mint, post office, treasury, supreme court, residences for ambassadors, all public offices, a capitol building for Congress, and the president's home (the White House).

Of the various places Wansey visited between Boston and Philadelphia, the pleasantest state to live in, in his opinion, was Connecticut; Worcester, Massachusetts, Springfield and Hartford, Connecticut, and Newark and Trenton, New Jersey, were among the pleasantest cities.

After Wansey returned to New York, he recorded further observations on that city. He was impressed with the extent of foreign trade with Europe and the Far East. For example, an American ship, the *Pegu,* went from Philadelphia to China, took on cargo, and returned within eleven months. Almost all the beer drunk in New York was brewed in and imported from London. The Americans preferred cider and whiskey. The general use of whiskey, Wansey thought, was "very pernicious." The British trade was by far the largest for exports and imports in all categories; for the year 1792, exports to Great Britain were valued at $9,363,416 and imports $15,285,428.

Other interesting statistics Wansey cited were the salaries paid President George Washington (5650 pounds) and Vice President John Adams (1125 pounds). The amount of the national debt in 1794 was $64,853,208. The population of the United States increased from 3,046,678 in 1774 to an estimated 5,250,690 in 1795; Virginia, the largest state, had 742,610 persons.

In a revealing appendix, "Literature," Wansey lists books reprinted in the United States and a separate list of original editions. The principal publishing centers were Boston, New York, and Philadelphia, and there was considerable emphasis on religion and history.

On July 2, 1794, Wansey boarded ship in New York for his return home. The fare was thirty guineas, in return for which the captain agreed "to find me in wine, porter, and provisions of all sorts, and with every necessary, except bedding and towels."

As souvenirs of his American travels, Wansey took back to

England two kinds of tortoises, a flying squirrel, and many kinds of shrubs and plants.

Wansey's overall judgment of American society was highly favorable. He concluded that "In these States you behold a certain plainness and simplicity of manners." Although many of the comforts of life were still lacking in the interior, he believed that America would be a happy solution for anyone not accustomed to luxury.

4. *A Year's Residence in the United States of America*

The art of controversial journalism and pamphleteering, insofar as America was concerned, was practically invented by William Cobbett.

Cobbett's often stormy career began early. He was the son of a small farmer at Farnham, Surrey, and the grandson of a day laborer. His adventures began when, at age fourteen, he ran away from home and found a job at Kew Gardens in London, and later served as a solicitor's clerk. Bored with that work, he joined the army and was sent first to Nova Scotia and then to New Brunswick, Canada. He taught himself grammar and writing. His ability was recognized by promotion to regimental sergeant-major, however the corruption that he discovered throughout the military service led him to obtain his discharge and to bring charges against his superior officers. These efforts were fruitless. After a period of residence in France, Cobbett decided in 1792 to leave for the United States, with the intention of becoming an American citizen. First in Wilmington, Delaware, and later in Philadelphia, he supported himself by teaching English to French refugees who were fleeing to the United States in large numbers because of the French Revolution.

Cobbett's first stay in America lasted eight years, during which he became a figure of national importance. In 1794 an incident occurred that launched him on his long career as a political writer. Joseph Priestley, the great scientist and Unitarian Radical, came in that year to settle in the United States after being driven by a mob from his home in Birmingham. Priestley was received with enthusiasm by the Republicans, who took advantage of the occasion to abuse England and to praise France. Cobbett, still loyal to his native Britain, was angered and proceeded to publish a pamphlet, signed "Peter Porcupine" and called *Observations on the Emigration of a Martyr to the Cause of Liberty,* which violently attacked Priestley and his admirers.

Thereafter, until his return to England in 1800, Cobbett was the most vehement and vitriolic writer on behalf of the English in the United States, producing a series of other essays under the pseudonym of Peter Porcupine that attacked the Republican party and all its doctrines as well as the French Revolution. Among his early pamphlets were *A Bone to Gnaw for the Democrats, A Kick for a Bite, The Cannibal's Progress* (an account of the horrors of the French Revolution), and a slanderous *Life of Tom Paine.* His pamphleteering was supplemented by a newspaper, *Porcupine's Gazette.* He defended Jay's Treaty, was critical of Edmund Randolph over the Fauchet Affair (Joseph Fauchet was the French minister who had accused Randolph of asking for money from France to influence the administration against Great Britain), and abused the French leaders. He wrote a bitter satire on the Jeffersonian doctrine of the equality of all men. Naturally, such writings stirred up powerful enemies against Cobbett, although he retained loyal friends.

Cobbett's downfall came when he attacked Dr. Benjamin Rush, well-known Democratic politician, and accused him of killing George Washington with his special "bleeding treatment" and of killing most of his other patients with excessive bloodletting. Cobbett was called into court three times to answer libel suits. In the third trial at the end of 1799 he was fined $5,000, which destroyed his printing business and bankrupted him. The following year he returned to England.

Back home, Cobbett's radical writings continued. At war with both Whigs and Tories, he served as spokesman for the dispossessed and suffering poor of rural England. He also denounced the harsh treatment of some mutinous militiamen, for which he was heavily fined and, accused of sedition, imprisoned for two years in Newgate prison.

In 1817, having accumulated huge debts amounting to 34,000 pounds, Cobbett again fled to America. There he acquired a small farm at Hyde Park near North Hempstead on Long Island. For the next two years he farmed and wrote *A Year's Residence in the United States.* The nature of *A Year's Residence* (actually two years in America) was quite different from Cobbett's previous writing. Because it was intended chiefly as a guide for emigrant farmers, he describes American farms, weather, and farming, as well as his experiments in rutabaga culture. He also offers generally complimentary observations on the character of the American people, whom he found to be industrious, prosperous, independent-spirited, hospitable, generally free of crime or dependence on charity, and materialistic, although too inclined to excessive use of alcohol. Cobbett admired the independence and prosperity of the American farmer, concluding that they were evidence of the benefits of political and religious freedom. As he declared, "A farmer here is not the poor dependent wretch that a Yeomanry-Cavalryman is, or that a Treason-Juryman is. A farmer here depends on nobody but *himself,* and on his own proper means; and if he is not at his ease and even rich, it must be his own fault."

During two months of travel in rural Pennsylvania, Cobbett was much impressed by the abundance and cheapness of rural life. Food was exceedingly plentiful. A Pennsylvania farmer usually had two houses, one large and one small, and a big stone barn. On the other hand, what Cobbett had heard of conditions in the Illinois country and farther west had convinced him that the rawness of the frontier made it unsuitable for emigrants. Utopians who dreamed of settlements in the wild and unexplored hinterland were ridiculed.

During the seventeen years that separated Cobbett's first and second stay in the United States, his views had undergone something of a revolution. He had become a confirmed democrat and an admirer of American institutions. He liked the Americans' practical approach to education, the fact that there was no established church, and a society in which almost every one earned his or her own living. The great advantages of American life, in Cobbett's judgment, were political, religious, and economic freedom. His principal criticisms were aimed at excessive drinking, unsettled conditions, and the squalor around each farmhouse or settlement outside cultivated areas.

After his farmhouse on Long Island burned in 1819, Cobbett returned to England, where he soon became an outstanding leader of working-class radical agitation. He was elected to Parliament in 1832, where he led a crusade against the Whig Government's Reform Act. His health broke down from strain and overwork, and he died in 1835.

Various attempts have been made to assess Cobbett's character. He was always extremely aggressive and pugnacious, quarrelling with both allies and opponents. Nevertheless, he made many firm friends. One biographer, G. D. H. Cole, pointed out that "He was intensely English, and, in his way, intensely patriotic; and it was this patriotism that roused him to the defense of his fellow-countrymen, trodden under by the oppressions of war and the twin revolutions in agriculture and industry whose devastating social effects he watched from phase to phase."

Another writer, Mary Elizabeth Clark, in her *Peter Porcupine in America: The Career of William Cobbett, 1792–1800,* concluded that Peter Porcupine was one of the forces that swung the young nation away from the monarchical and aristocratic tradition toward Jeffersonian democracy. During his eight years in the United States, in the course of his first story, Cobbett became one of the most potent sources molding public opinion in the new republic. He may rightly be considered one of the founders of a party press.

5. *Travels to the West of the Allegheny Mountains into Ohio, Kentucky and Tennessee*

In choosing his own career, François Michaux followed in his father's footsteps. André Michaux, the father, was a distinguished French botanist who had traveled widely in Europe and the Near East, ending with ten years devoted to the study of American botany and the publication of two books on the subject. Among other activities, he established a botanic garden outside Charleston, and it was there that his son, François, frequently visited to study forestry. The son had received a thorough education in forestry and medicine; his research eventually led to publication in 1810 of his classic work on trees, *The North American Sylva.*

François Michaux docked at Charleston in October 1801 to begin an exploratory trip into the frontier country beyond the Alleghenies. Charleston, however, was in the grip of its annual yellow fever epidemic. After recovering from an attack himself, Michaux visited New York and Philadelphia. Then, in June 1802, at age thirty-two, he started westward through Pennsylvania. His detailed journal provides many fresh insights into pioneer settlements.

Housing was an aspect of American society that Michaux explored. Where and how did the people live? In Philadelphia, he found that homes were built of brick; in nearby towns and country places, half or more were built of wood. One-third of the inhabitants lived in log houses as distances increased beyond seventy or eighty miles of the sea, in the central and southern states and especially west of the Allegheny Mountains. Construction was simple, and two men could finish a log house in four or five days, using no nails. Two doors took the place of windows and moved on wooden hinges. Space between trunks of trees was filled with clay, but carelessly done so light shined through. The board floor was raised one or two feet above the ground. Furniture was generally limited to two large beds for the entire family. There were feather beds, but no mattresses.

Accommodations for travelers on the road were generally mediocre, Michaux reported. Inns were numerous, but very bad everywhere except in the principal towns. Quantities of rum, brandy, and whiskey were available and consumed. In fact, Michaux found "A passion for spirituous liquors is one of the features that characterize the country people belonging to the interior of the United States. This passion is so strong that they desert their homes every now and then to get drunk in public houses."

Meals served in the inns were equally unsatisfactory: Breakfast included very indifferent tea and coffee still worse, with small slices of fried ham "to which eggs and broiled chicken were sometimes added; at dinner, a piece of salt beef, roasted fowls; in the evening, coffee, tea and ham. There were several beds in each of the rooms where travelers slept and rarely were there clean sheets."

Pittsburgh had about 400 houses, principally brick, at the time of Michaux's visit. He pronounced the Pittsburgh air as "very salubrious," not afflicted with the fever epidemics common in southern states, and free of mosquitoes. The city had become an important commercial center. Goods were carried from Philadelphia in large covered wagons drawn by four horses, two abreast. There was also active shipping by barges between Pittsburgh and New Orleans, a distance of 1,500 miles that took forty to fifty days for a passage.

After passing through Pittsburgh, Michaux and a companion bought a pirogue, an Indian canoe, and embarked on the Ohio at Wheeling, West Virginia. For the next ten days they traveled through magnificent natural scenery. Michaux's fascination with trees is apparent in his description of the shore along the river:

"Willows from fifteen to eighteen feet in height, the drooping branches and foliage of which form a pleasing contrast to the sugar maples, red maples, and ash trees situated immediately above. The latter, in return, are overlooked by palms, poplars, beeches, magnolias of the highest elevation . . . the enormous branches of which overshadow the river."

The three new western states that Michaux visited were growing rapidly in population. Thirty years previously, there had been about 3,000 inhabitants. By 1802, that number had increased to 400,000. Crossing the Ohio to Charter Creek, Kentucky, the travelers spent the night at "an indifferent inn" where there was but one bed for wayfarers. Late arrivals wrapped themselves in a rug and slept on the floor.

Michaux noted that people along the Ohio spent most of their time in deer and bear hunting, which left them little time to cultivate their farms. A majority lived in miserable log huts without windows and so small that there was hardly room for more than two beds. The main crop was Indian corn, and the majority of the inhabitants ate only bread made of corn, baked into eight-to-ten-pound loaves. More than one-half of the people who lived on the borders of the Ohio were first settlers. They were a restless folk, constantly moving west on the pretext of looking for richer land or a milder climate. Newer settlers usually built more substantial houses and diversified their crops by adding other grain, hemp, and tobacco. Rich pastures enabled them to grow large domestic herds and flocks; Kentucky became famous for breeding fine horses and horned cattle. Hogs, kept by everybody, were the most numerous of the domestic animals and ran wild in forests.

Michaux observed that nearly all the inhabitants of Kentucky were originally natives of Virginia and had preserved the manners of Virginians, such as a passion for gambling and for spirituous liquors. Public houses were always crowded, and violent crimes not infrequent. Women seldom worked in the fields, but were attentive to domestic duties including spinning hemp or cotton into linen for their families' use.

Methodists and Baptists were most numerous among religious sects. Sundays were carefully observed, and in summers there were assemblies of two or three thousand people to hear sermons. These meetings lasted for several days, during which the preachers' sermons would rouse the congregations to emotional excesses. Schools were tax-supported, and children were kept in them until they had learned reading, writing, and arithmetic.

After exploring Tennessee, Michaux recrossed the Alleghenies and toured Georgia and the Carolinas before returning to Charleston. Much cotton was cultivated in the lowlands of that area, a process greatly expedited by the invention of Eli Whitney's cotton gin in 1794. The machine could separate 300 to 400 pounds of cotton from the seed in a day in contrast to the old laborious hand method that yielded not more than thirty pounds. Charleston was a marketing center, where cotton, tobacco, hams, salt butter, stag and bear skins, and cattle were marketed, and coarse hardware, tea, coffee, powder, sugar, coarse cloths, and fine linens were bought.

The best rice plantations were in the great swamps, where water was plentiful. Corn was cultivated on all the plantations and was destined chiefly for feeding slaves, each of whom was allowed two pounds per day nine months out of the year. During the remaining three months, they were fed yams. Agricultural labor was performed by blacks throughout the low country. In other areas, they were better fed and better treated.

Michaux sailed for France in March 1803. In later years, he retired to a country estate in France, where he lived on until 1855.

6. *A Journal of Travels into the Arkansas Territory During the Year 1819*

Thomas Nuttall, formerly a printer's apprentice from Liverpool, came to Philadelphia in 1808 at age twenty-two. There he became associated with the city's most distinguished figures in scientific and intellectual life, notably members of the American Philosophical Society and the Academy of Natural Sciences of Philadelphia.

Before leaving England, Nuttall had grown fascinated with botany, had gone on botanizing excursions with a better-educated young friend in Liverpool, and had studied Latin, Greek, and French in preparation for further botanical research.

The Lewis and Clark expedition had sent back a rich collection of natural science specimens from Fort Mandan on the Upper Missouri in 1805 to be described by a pioneer botanist of the time, Benjamin Smith Barton. Barton, in turn, signed a contract with Nuttall to retrace the Lewis and Clark route and to devote himself to further "collecting animals, vegetables, minerals, Indian curiosities, etc."

The route mapped out by Nuttall was primarily traveled by boat and took him in 1818 from Philadelphia to Pittsburgh, down the Ohio River to its mouth, then down the Mississippi to the mouth of the Arkansas and to eastern Oklahoma—a journey that extended for more than half a continent. The area traversed included the Near Southwest fifteen years after the Louisiana Purchase, a region that was going through explosive changes marked by conflicts with Spain and Mexico, Indian migrations and wars, and increasing white settlement.

On his first journey beyond the Appalachians, Nuttall began to find completely unknown plant species. Thereafter, botanical exploration became the controlling passion of his life. His early observations were incorporated in 1834 in the first botanical work of broad scope published in America, *Collections towards Three Flora of the Territory of Arkansas.* No other botanist collected as many new kinds of plants within what is now the United States, or saw so much of it in primeval condition. Nuttall wrote the first ornithology of North America, three editions of which were published before 1900.

Nuttall was an acute observer. He had a nearly insatiable interest in Indian antiquities and the contemporary life of the aborigines. In the course of his travels, Nuttall became acquainted with a number of southwestern Indian tribes: the Chickasaws, Quapaws, Cherokees, Osages, Choctaws, Shawnees, and Delawares. The Indians were generally averse to agriculture and systematic labor, and principally dependent upon hunting for bare subsistence.

The Indians' cattle in the Arkansas territory were generally left to roam at large, except for an occasional ration of salt and a few ears of corn. They stayed in reasonably good condition by eating cane and sagebrush. Horned cattle increased and fattened without any labor or attention. Horses, too, had become naturalized; they were small, hardy, and able to exist entirely upon cane or grass.

Nuttall describes the folk customs that prevailed among various Indian tribes. For example, some groups, such as the Ozarks, used artificial methods to remove all surplus hair from their bodies, plucking out their eyebrows, shaving their beards, and leaving only a small scalp upon the crowns of their heads. Every family had a guardian spirit chosen for its wisdom, utility, or power—for example, a snake, buffalo, owl, raven, or eagle—to provide sacred charms. After the death of a warrior or hunter, food was placed on his grave for a reasonable length of time. Some Indians had developed the art of thievery to an expert level in preference to hard labor, according to legend. Even a blind Indian whom Nuttall met had become an accomplished thief.

The Osage practiced many superstitions, often stressing the importance of smoking as a religious ceremony. Before going out to war, they would raise the pipe towards heaven or the sun to implore the Great Spirit's aid in stealing horses, destroying their enemies, and or gaining revenge.

Nuttall and some of his companions as well as numerous Indians were afflicted with the malaria and yellow fever raging at the time, and there were a number of deaths among the Indians. Nuttall himself was often too weak to walk, or even to sit on a horse. In the 1820s, it was estimated that 20,000 inhabitants in the New Orleans area were stricken by yellow fever.

Slavery was still dominant along vast stretches of the Mississippi in Nuttall's time, but he recommended the gradual abolition of this institution even before the coming of the Civil War.

In 1822, Nuttall became director of the botanical garden of Harvard University, but resigned in 1834 to accompany the Nathanial J. Wyeth expedition to the Pacific coast. Samuel Eliot Morrison wrote in *Three Centuries of Harvard* that Nuttall was "easily the first man of science in Augustan Harvard."

Originally, Nuttall had hoped to remain permanently in America, but at the end of 1841 he reluctantly left for his native England, where he died in 1859. His departure ended a distinguished record of scientific exploration and of solid accomplishment in advancing the knowledge of American plants, birds and other animal groups, minerals, and geology. In a brief autobiography of his life in America, Nuttall wrote:

> Thirty-four years ago, I left England to explore the natural history of the United States. In the ship Halcyon I arrived at the shores of the New World; and after a boisterous and dangerous passage, our dismasted vessel entered the Capes of the Delaware in the month of April. The beautiful robing of forest scenery, now bursting into vernal life, was exchanged for the monotony of the dreary ocean, and sad sickness of the sea. As we sailed up the Delaware my eyes were rivetted on the landscape with intense admiration. All was new!—and life, like that season, was then full of hope and enthusiasm. The

forests apparently unbroken, in their primeval solitude and repose spread themselves on either side as we passed placidly along. The extending vista of dark Pines gave an air of deep sadness to the wilderness. . . .

Scenes like these have little attraction for ordinary life. But to the naturalist it is far otherwise; privations to him are cheaply purchased if he may roam over the wild domain of primeval nature. . . .

How often have I realized the poet's buoyant hopes amid these solitary rambles through interminable forests! For thousands of miles my chief converse has been in the wilderness with the spontaneous productions of nature; and the study of these objects and their contemplation has been to me a source of constant delight.

The fervid curiosity led me to the bank of the Ohio, through the dark forests and brakes of the Mississippi, to the distant lakes of the northern frontier; through the wilds of Florida; far up the Red River and the Missouri, and through the territory of Arkansaw. And now across the arid plains of the Far West, beyond the steppes of the Rocky Mountains, down the Oregon to the extended shores of the Pacific, across the distant ocean to that famous group, the Sandwich Islands, where Cook at length fell a sacrifice to his temerity. And here for the first time I beheld the beauties of a tropical vegetation; . . . an elysian land where nature offers spontaneous good to man. . . .

Leaving this favoured region of perpetual mildness, I now arrived on the shores of California, at Monterrey. The early spring (March) had already spread out its varied carpet of flowers; all of them had to me the charm of novelty, and many were adorned with the most brilliant and varied hues. . . . The scenery was mountainous and varied, one vast wilderness, neglected and uncultivated; and the cattle appeared as wild as the bison of the prairies. . . .

After a perilous passage around Cape Horn, the dreary extremity of South America, amid mountains of ice which opposed our progress in unusual array, we arrived again at the shores of the Atlantic. Once more I hailed those delightful scenes of nature with which I had been so long associated. I rambled again through the shade of the Atlantic forests, or culled some rare productions of Flora in their native wilds. But the "oft-told tale" approaches to its close and I must now bid a long adieu to the 'New World,' its sylvan scenes, its mountains, wilds, and plains; and henceforth, in the evening of my career, I return almost an exile, to the land of my nativity.

His leading biographer, Jeanette Graustein, comments that "Nuttall's manifold advancements of the natural history of North America are truly unique in accomplishment and in their spirit of complete dedication."

7. *The Domestic Manners of the Americans*

Frances Trollope is remembered as the author of the most prejudiced and most widely discussed of all travel books on the United States, *The Domestic Manners of the Americans,* and also as the mother of two prominent novelists, Anthony and Thomas Trollope.

Misfortunes dogged the Trollope family from the beginning. Trollope's husband, Thomas, was a barrister whose every financial venture was a disaster until he ended in total bankruptcy. With a view to ending their run of bad luck and improving the family's financial situation, Frances Trollope and three of her seven children came to America in 1827.

Her poor judgment and lack of practicality were early shown by her scheme to establish a bazaar in Cincinnati, then a frontier community, for the sale of fancy goods and knick-knacks such as pincushions, pepper boxes, and pocket knives. To house this enterprise, Trollope designed what another English traveler described as the "most absurd, ugly, and ridiculous" building in town, at an expense far beyond her means. It was constructed of brick, had Gothic windows, Grecian pillars, a Turkish dome, and was ornamented with Egyptian devices. The venture proved a complete failure because of lack of customers, and was finally taken over by creditors. Trollope then proceeded on to New York as the first stage of her return to England. In the years that followed Trollope's departure, the huge, grotesque building that she left behind in Cincinnati was used as an inn, a dancing school, a Presbyterian church, a theater, a mechanics' institute, and a military hospital.

Trollope's experiences in Cincinnati had soured her disposition and left her in a frame of mind decidedly unfriendly to Americans. She had found the rather crude society of Cincinnati disagreeable and unacceptable. During her two years there, she had had ample opportunity to observe American manners and customs. In her eyes, there was practically nothing to commend. She made notes on everything—oddities of speech, dress, and politics, of eating and love-making and housekeeping, the curious manners of the parlor, the ballroom, the market place, and the camp meeting. In particular, Trollope found the tobacco habit and the constant spitting most repulsive. She also objected to the way Americans ate watermelon, their leaving garbage disposal to wandering hogs, the lack of "elegancies," the presumptuous behavior of servants, the scenes at revivalist meetings, the separation of the sexes at parties, and a variety of other minor matters.

Frances Trollope was quite unfitted by temperament and rearing to face back-country living. When she arrived in Cincinnati, she was already forty-seven, extremely fond of parties and good society, and accustomed to the amenities of genteel European living. She had no knowledge of business affairs and very limited funds. Nothing in her previous career and upbringing prepared her for her Cincinnati undertaking.

Before embarking on her return voyage home, Trollope visited several other cities, about which her comments were generally more favorable. She found the approach to Baltimore beautiful; she was "delighted with the whole aspect of Washington; light, cheerful and airy, it reminded me of our fashionable watering-places; Philadelphia was too strict and sanctimonious." New York drew her highest praise, especially the "patrician class" hosts for whose hospitality she was properly appreciative.

In 1832, a year after she returned to England, Frances Trollope's *The Domestic Manners of the Americans* was published, bringing her instant fame. She was the literary lion of the season, and her financial woes were temporarily resolved. Although a late-starter, she was amazingly prolific. Between the ages of fifty and seventy-five, she produced a total of 114 volumes, including four novels that dealt with American life.

A tremendous uproar followed United States publication of Trollope's highly critical *Domestic Manners*. Everyone read the book while roundly damning it for unfairness, ill nature, and bias. One edition after another rolled off the press to meet the demand. The author had given Americans ample cause for resentment.

Among Trollope's major criticisms was that Americans showed a "total and universal want of manners, both in males and females." They were too inquisitive, boring, uncultivated, lacking in humor, and egotistical. In her opinion, public behavior was appalling. She saw a woman suckling a baby at the theater. Men sat at the edge of boxes, with their backs to the audience, or sprawled with their feet propped up. She felt that American women were quite handsome when young, but their posture was bad and they had scrawny figures. Men were worse: "I never saw an American man walk or stand well; they are nearly all hollow chested and round shouldered." Table manners, Trollope felt, were especially offensive:

> The total want of all the usual courtesies of the table . . . the loathsome spitting from the contamination of which it was absolutely impossible to protect our dresses; the frightful manner of feeding with their knives, till the whole blade seemed to enter into the mouth; and the still more frightful manner of cleaning the teeth afterwards with a pocket knife, soon forced us to feel that the dinner hour was to be any thing rather than an hour of enjoyment.

Trollope concluded also that, except for blacks, Americans had no ear for music: "I scarcely ever heard a white American go through an air without being out of tune before the end of it."

She was especially critical of Americans' contempt for law: "Trespass, assault, robbery, nay, even murder, are often committed without the slightest attempt at legal interference." There was general indifference to the rights of slaves and Indians. In her words: "You will see them with one hand hoisting the cup of liberty, and with the other flogging their slaves. You will see them one hour lecturing their mob on the indefensible rights of man, and the next driving from their homes the children of the soil [Indians] whom they have bound themselves to protect by the most solemn treaties."

Thomas Jefferson was an object of sharpest criticism; she held him responsible for the foolish and dangerous proposition that all men were created equal, despite which he kept slaves and was rumored to have fathered children by his female slaves.

In her final chapter, Trollope sums up with a declaration that—except for a "small patrician band" of well-bred and congenial people—Americans were dull, brutal, and arrogant. Too, they were highly sensitive to any word of criticism, producing an atmosphere uncompatible for a cultured European. In Trollope's prejudiced view, Americans had inherited a great country, but were destroying it and ruining their own morals. She warned England against the "jarring tumult and universal degradation which invariably follow the wild scheme of placing all the power of the state in the hands of the populace."

The contemporary opinion was that *Domestic Manners* had been written by an ill-informed woman who had suffered unfortunate experiences in the United States. Coming so soon after the Revolution and the War of 1812, Americans thought that they detected a jealous, disdainful resentment on the part of the mother country.

On the other hand, as time passed, it was recognized that there was truth and some justification for Trollope's acerbic remarks. In an objective study, *As Others See Us,* John Graham Brooks decided that the overall effect was salutary: "Even the saucy Mrs. Trollope, whose every page left a smart, actually modified some of our habits. Men who sprawled in their shirt-sleeves in a theatre box, or thrust a foot over the railing in a gallery, about 1840, often heard the word 'Trollope! Trollope!' shouted in the audience . . . much in these criticisms entered into our common thought and helped to form that self-criticism which makes the better possible."

A similar comment was offered by Mark Twain, who said that

"Poor candid Mrs. Trollope lived three years in this civilization of ours, in the body of it—not on the surface of it, as was the case with most of the foreign tourists of her day. She knew her subject well, and she set it forth fairly and squarely without any weak ifs, ands or buts. She deserved gratitude—but it is an error to suppose she got it."

8. *Travels in North America in the Years 1827 and 1828*

Not even the bitter pens of Harriet Martineau and Frances Trollope aroused the wrath and resentment of the American people as did Captain Basil Hall's three-volume account of his travels in the United States and Canada in 1827-28. He was regarded as an arch traitor to the generous hospitality he and his wife and infant daughter received during their leisurely 10,000 mile tour over most of the known territory of the United States. Hall himself mentions repeatedly the kindness shown him during the long tour. All houses were open to him, and he was treated as a friend of the family, especially if he carried letters of introduction to an American household. One commentator noted that the Hall family never received the least incivility or affront in the course of their travels.

Furthermore, the captain claimed, "Probably there seldom was a traveler who visited a foreign land in a more kindly spirit. I was really desirous of seeing everything relating to the people, country, and institutions in the most favorable light."

Hall, the son of a Scotch geologist, entered the British navy at the age of thirteen, saw active service during the Napoleonic wars, accompanied Lord Amherst's embassy to China, was made a fellow of the Royal Society on the basis of his ethnographical writings, interviewed Napoleon at St. Helena, and was stationed on the Pacific coast of South America and Mexico in 1820-22. With such a background, Hall believed himself fully competent to judge American institutions and to speak dogmatically on everything that he saw.

Americans felt differently. The prevailing view was that the Tory government of England had sent Hall "to depreciate republican institutions, and to repress the growing spirit of freedom at home." Frances Trollope, who came along a few years later, reported that Hall's book "was read in city, town, village and hamlet, steamboat, and stage-coach, and a sort of war-whoop was sent forth unprecedented in my recollection upon any occasion whatever." She was told that the work did not contain one word of truth from beginning to end.

A more balanced assessment comes from the American historian Allan Nevins, whose judgment was that "the author was a bluff, honest, clear-headed, practical-minded mariner, whose High-Tory prejudices were all inimical to the crude democratic society he found in America, who had little tact with which to smooth his way, and who candidly sets down his displeasure with all that he disliked." Hall examined American institutions, religion, manners, habits, politics, business, and modes of life and applied English standards to them. Any variation from the English mode was likely to win his disapproval. He seemed unable to remain silent whenever he saw anything to criticize, and he was frequently a thorn in the flesh to people that he met.

The itinerary for Hall's travel followed a pattern set by most mid-nineteenth-century travelers in America. He landed in New York, and his first volume treats his tour through that state to Niagara and Canada. The second volume covers New England and the Middle States as far south as Baltimore, and the third is devoted to the South and the Mississippi.

The chief tenets Hall belabored were Americans' refusal to accept the practice of primogeniture, whereby the eldest son became sole heir to an estate, in favor of the more popular principle of equal distribution of property; the universality of electoral suffrage; equality of popular rights and privileges; "and all the other transatlantic devices for the improvement of society."

In New York, at the beginning of his travels, Hall was impressed by the huge amount of food served by the large hotels. Every day at three o'clock an immense table d'hote would be spread for guests not living in the house. As many as a hundred persons would be seated at a table. A smaller and less public dinner was served for the hotel's guests. Those who wanted to have their meals privately were charged $2 a day extra. The captain's attempts at conversation and sociability were rejected by other guests, who were solely intent on gobbling up their food.

Hall commended the management and accomplishments of several New York institutions that he visited: the House of Refuge for juvenile delinquents, a similar establishment for girls, the high schools (one for boys, another for girls), and a school for the education of black and mulatto children. Although slavery had been abolished in New York, Hall noted that "a black man meets with no real and effective sympathy on the part of the white lords of the creation . . . let a negro be ever so industrious or well-informed, still he seems stamped for degradation."

Two features of life in New York that Hall criticized were the absence of wigs and gowns among justices of the New York Supreme Court, which he felt caused a loss of dignity, and the inferior quality of art in public galleries.

Hall was disillusioned by a visit to the New York state legislature, where the discussion struck him as "rather juvenile," and the speeches "full of set phrases and rhetorical flourishes." Members were chiefly farmers, shopkeepers, and country lawyers who had limited education and lacked legislative experience. A fatal flaw in the system, as seen by Hall, was the rapid turnover in the composition of legislative bodies. As soon as members become somewhat familiar with their duties, fresh elections would be scheduled, old members thrown out, and new ones voted in. He found the same fault in the U.S. Congress, as a consequence of which "those persons best fitted by their education, habits of business, knowledge, and advantageous situation of whatever sort, for performing, efficiently, the duties of statesmen, are excluded from the national councils." The American system compared unfavorably with England's, where elections were held on the average about every four years; "in America the electioneering spirit never dies."

On May 29, 1827, the Hall family boarded a Hudson River steamer to start their travels north. A stop was made at Sing Sing to inspect the state prison, the administration of which was rated excellent. In Hall's opinion, however, "the convicts who are sentenced to confinement in the state prisons of America, are chiefly such as in England would be either executed or banished."

As a military man, Hall discussed the work of the military academy at West Point at some length. His verdict in general was favorable, although the captain remarked that "according to European rules, the cadets were remarkably deficient in that erect carriage and decided, firm gait, which gives a military air."

Albany, the state capital, was found to be in the midst of a commercial boom because of the recent completion of the Erie Canal, of which Albany was the eastern terminus.

Hall digressed at this stage of his account for some observations on the American character. He found Americans' most striking feature to be their "constant habit of praising themselves, their institutions, and their country." As a corollary, Americans "were eternally on the defensive, and gave us to understand that they suspected us of a design to find fault, at times when nothing on earth was farther from our thoughts."

Hall commented with some amusement on the American practice of attaching classical names to what he described as "these mushroom towns in the wilderness," such as Troy, Ithaca, Rome, Syracuse, Utica, Cicero, and Homer, as well as London, Dublin, and Edinburgh. Hall also found the predominance of two-pronged instead of three-pronged forks a minor dining annoyance, because the instrument made it impossible for him to pick up peas or rice.

By the end of June, the Halls reached Niagara Falls, which "infinitely exceeded our anticipations." After several days of sightseeing there, they continued on to Canada. The last fourteen chapters of his first volume, which cover from July to September 1827, are devoted to Canadian travels.

An evil rising out of too much democracy that was dangerous, in Hall's opinion, was Americans' excessive use of intoxicating liquors; "it threatens to sap the foundation of everything good in America—political and domestic," with consequences worse than yellow fever or slavery. Hall was "perfectly astonished at the extent of intemperance," although he saw few men completely intoxicated.

During a visit to Harvard University, Hall went leisurely from class to class and found the students busily engaged and receiving much encouragement from their professors. He saw the library, which he was told was "very rich in valuable and rare books." Many public schools in Massachusetts were maintained by taxation, and Bostonians were proud of this system. Hall felt that such a plan resembled charity in the case of poor people's children, but was assured that general education was essential to the republican form of government. Wealthier families generally sent their children to private schools. Few students could be persuaded to remain in school or college long enough to gain a thorough classical education, however.

In New Haven, Hall was introduced to the famous lexicographer Noah Webster, and a lively dialogue followed. Hall was concerned with what he considered the corruption of the English language by Americanisms. Webster insisted that "it is quite impossible to stop the progress of language—it is like the course of the Mississippi . . . it possesses a momentum quite irresistible." The captain responded, "surely such innovations are to be deprecated . . . there are words enough already; and it only confuses matters, and hurts the cause of letters to introduce such words." Webster, of course, disagreed.

Hall's long digression on the American political system was inspired by the national election of November 1827. He describes the history, theory, and principal features of the U.S. government. The framers of the Constitution, he believed, intended to establish a republic, not a democracy—a fact lost sight of with the passage of time. A democracy, he felt, does not bring the most qualified men into power nor retain their services long—a sentiment echoed later to some extent by Alexander Mackay and Sir James Bryce.

Turning from what he regarded as the rather disagreeable subject of politics, Hall went on to investigate the state of science and literature in the United States. He made pleasant contacts with the Lyceum of Natural History in New York and the American Philosophical Society in Philadelphia. Like other foreign authors, he deplored the lack of copyright protection. Low prices appeared the main aim of American publishers, the probable explanation for the "miserable paper, printing, and binding" of nearly all reprinted books.

To conclude his second volume, Hall analyzed the American judicial system, with its good and bad aspects. He also mentioned the disgusting American habit of chewing tobacco and constant spitting—a practice he condemned as ungentlemanly and abominable, and one that would not be tolerated in Europe.

In the third and concluding volume of the account of his travels, Captain Hall headed south, beginning with a month's stay in Washington, where there was an opportunity to study Congress in session. He noted that speakers in the Senate, "Instead of sticking to the point, . . . all wandered off into what is much miscalled eloquence, and entertained the House with long strings of truisms and common-places," with occasional slaps at England. He met President John Quincy Adams and "several military and naval officers of distinction." As Hall stated after a visit to the New York State legislature, the business of Congress "is greatly retarded and embarrassed by the large number of new and inexperienced members, who come in every second year."

In Washington, Hall witnessed his first slave sale. Like other foreign visitors, he was shocked by that "humiliating" spectacle in the nation's capital.

American military discipline came in for Hall's criticism after he visited Fortress Monroe in Virginia. An act of Congress had abolished the old method of punishing offenses in the American army by flogging. No other system of punishment, in Hall's opinion, was as effective, and because flogging was discontinued, he felt that "the discipline of the troops had been gradually declining, and the soldiers becoming discontented."

While traveling through other southern states and seeing slaves laboring under various conditions, Hall had frequent occasion to discuss the slavery system with planters and political leaders. Some strongly defended the practice as essential to southern agriculture, others favored abolition. Hall himself could find little good to say about what he concluded to be an evil institution.

Among the worst long-range consequences of slave labor was that it wore out formerly rich land, exhausted by nonrotation of crops such as tobacco and corn. Because of this fact, Hall thought it likely that slavery would eventually die a natural death.

Hall's later travels took him to the Great Dismal Swamp in North Carolina, to Charleston, through Georgia and Alabama, on a visit to a tribe of Creek Indians, and to New Orleans and the Mississippi. Before returning to England in July 1828, there were also stops in Louisville, St. Louis, and Cincinnati. He and his family had been absent from England for more than fifteen months.

Hall's final chapter is devoted to an extended debate between himself and a supposedly representative, unnamed American. Hall defends the monarchical tradition; the advantages of distinctions in ranks; the virtues of having an established church with a close alliance between church and state; and placing public affairs in the hands of the ablest men in the country instead of constant rotation by frequent elections. The American naturally takes issue on every point.

Hall concludes, "I have had the pleasure of becoming acquainted with many persons in America, whose good will and good opinion I hope I shall never lose." Such noble sentiments, however, did not soothe ruffled American feelings. Two noteworthy American protests followed publication of Hall's book in 1829: One was a long review in the *North American Review,* the other a refutation published in 1830 titled *Captain Hall in America by an American,* which later proved to be by Richard Biddle. The first review attacked Hall's character, whereas Biddle was concerned with correcting errors and misleading statements.

9. *Democracy in America*

Alexis de Tocqueville's *Democracy in America* has been rated as the greatest work ever written on one country by the citizen of another. The author's primary interest was the subject of democracy, not America, and he chose the United States for study because it was the first major democracy in the modern world.

Tocqueville was no liberal nor democrat by disposition. His family belonged to the oldest Norman nobility and had suffered the worst terrors of the French Revolution. A number of his ancestors had been sent to the guillotine. Tocqueville's own sympathies were strongly oriented toward aristocracy, but he had come to the conclusion that democracy was the inevitable political development in the years to come. He determined, therefore, to find out for himself what a democratic regime had to contribute to the cause of liberty and to a solution of the problems confronting his beloved France, then still in a state of turmoil from the Revolution and from the aftermath of the Napoleonic Wars.

Tocqueville's opportunity came in 1831, at the age of twenty-six, when he and his young friend Gustave de Beaumont were commissioned by the Minister of the Interior to study the penitentiary system of the United States for any features that might be applicable to French prisons.

The official mission was conscientiously completed, although it was incidental to Tocqueville's main concern. Over a period of nine months, he and Beaumont traveled widely through New England, Canada, New York, Philadelphia, Baltimore, Cincinnati,

Tennessee, New Orleans, and Washington. Tocqueville came to know at first hand the geography of the United States, with its often spectacular scenery and vast distances. He experienced the climate in all seasons, crossed mountains in snowstorms, traveled in steamboats, and explored the great forests. Perhaps more important, he met pioneer settlers and came to have an unusual understanding of the frontier. He studied the westward movement of the population, observed the first emigrants, watched the retreat of the Indians, and noticed the building of roads and the organization of territorial governments. He became acquainted with various regions of the country, being conscious of their strong contrasts, racial problems, and economic rivalries.

Tocqueville was fascinated by the America that he found. "I confess," he wrote, "that in America I saw more than America; I sought the image of democracy itself, with its inclinations, its character, its prejudices, and its passions, in order to learn what we have to fear or to hope from its progress." It is astonishing that Tocqueville was able to grasp the essentials of American civilization so thoroughly and to write with so much depth and penetration after a visit of only nine months. Part of the explanation is that he was an extraordinarily keen observer who kept careful notebooks on every aspect of his travels. As George Wilson Pierson stated in his *Tocqueville and Beaumont in America,* there was not a single chapter in *Democracy in America* "that did not draw most of its basic ideas and many illustrative details directly from the study that he had made, personally, in the United States, on the spot." The notebooks were first translated and published by George Lawrence in 1960, in a work titled *Journey to America.*

Tocqueville found the day-to-day business of American life absorbing. He considers architecture, literature, social manners, ways of speaking, the theater, equality between the sexes, wages, and the status of officers in democratic armies. He was particularly interested in the development of communications, and devotes much space to the delivery of the mails and to river traffic. One of the steamboats on which he traveled sank during the voyage, and another one ran aground on a Mississippi sandbank. Americans, he felt, paid too little attention to dress, served dinner courses in the wrong order, and had no feeling for their language; their orators were ridiculously pompous, whereas their cities and society were dull in part because there was no American aristocracy and no class distinctions.

Tocqueville spent much time visiting frontier areas, fascinated with the growth of western cities and the ever-receding frontier—a phenomenon made famous years later by the historian Frederick Jackson Turner. In these pioneer communities, Tocqueville found the epitome of classlessness, democratization, and complete individualism. He found Americans, especially those in the western states, to be a deeply religious people, a reaction, he reasoned, to excessive materialism.

The first part of *Democracy in America* appeared in 1835, when Tocqueville was thirty, and the second half five years later. It is evident that the author was both attracted and repelled by what he had seen. Democracy as practiced here, he concluded, was full of contradictions: liberty threatened by the tyranny of the majority, widespread educational opportunities, and offset by too much standardization of opinion; respect for authority and personal rights was offset by a spirit of irresponsibility. Nevertheless, two beliefs were deeply ingrained in the American people: equality and majority rule.

In Tocqueville's interpretation of America, one grand theme predominates: the concept of a new society founded upon equality among its members. As he commented, "The more I studied the social conditions of America the more I saw that this equality of conditions was the vital fact round which every individual circumstance seemed to revolve, and I found it again and again as the one central point to which all my observations tended to return."

Tocqueville believed that the matter of centralization versus decentralization had a vital bearing on the success of democratic institutions. The American experiment in democracy gained its greatest strength, he thought, from local and individual participation in government represented, for example, by the New England town meetings that he had attended.

A prophetic insight into the dangers of slavery was shown by

Tocqueville. If America was to encounter serious future problems, the troubles would "be brought about by the presence of the black race on the soil of the United States." He foresaw that slavery must be abolished, but that freedom would not end racial prejudice or social troubles.

The true prophet's voice is heard again in Tocqueville's observations on the future roles of America and Russia: "There are at the present time two great nations in the world which seem to tend toward the same end, although they started from different points. I allude to the Russians and the Americans. . . . The principal instrument of the Anglo-American is freedom; of the Russian servitude. Their starting point is different, and their courses are not the same, yet each of them seems to be marked out by the will of Heaven to sway the destinies of half the globe."

Other matters treated by Tocqueville are worthy of special mention: the advantages and disadvantages of democracy, the influence of democracy upon intellectual development, the difficulties in recruiting men of superior ability for public office (a theme explored some years later by Sir James Bryce), the need for some measure of government control over large industries, and the importance of the press as "the chiefest democratic instrument of freedom."

Although unsympathetic to democratic government in some of its less attractive aspects, Tocqueville concluded that "the progress of democracy seems irresistible, because it is the most uniform, the most ancient, and the most permanent tendency which is to be found in history."

Democracy in America was one of the most influential books of the nineteenth century. It provided strong reinforcement for liberal convictions that political equality and democratic self-government were inevitable. Much of what Tocqueville wrote about American political institutions at the time of his visit to the United States has become outdated, but his work is a monument in the intellectual history of the West, helping to shape the thought and actions of succeeding generations of political leaders and scientists.

After his return to France, Tocqueville entered the Chamber of Deputies in 1839, but achieved no political prominence until the time of the Second Republic, when he served as foreign minister from June to October 1849. He retired from active politics after Louis Napoleon's coup d'etat. The remainder of his life was devoted to a history of the French Revolution and the First Empire, but he completed only an introductory study.

Frances Anne (Fanny) Kemble, 1809–93

10. *Journal of a Residence on a Georgian Plantation in 1838–1839*

Financial considerations were the principal motive for the cele-brated actress Fanny Kemble's first visit to America. Her father, Charles Kemble, also an actor, was owner-manager of Covent Garden. Kemble was phenomenally successful as an actress in her father's company, but the theater was heavily burdened with debts when he became manager. Bankruptcy was imminent, so the Kembles determined to come to America in an effort to recoup their fortunes.

Fanny Kemble was the last of a great dynasty of English actors and actresses—the daughter, granddaughter, and great-granddaughter of some of the most famous names on the London stage for several generations. Her debut came in 1829 at the age of nineteen in the role of Juliet. Theaters were crowded wherever she performed.

In August 1832, Kemble and her father sailed for New York. Again the Kemble magic fascinated packed houses in New York, Philadelphia, Boston, Baltimore, and Washington. Strangely, though, she hated acting and yearned to leave the theater. Her escape route was a disastrous marriage in 1834 to Pierce Butler.

Butler was the grandson of a southern planter, wealthy from his plantations, prominent in Philadelphia society, blond, magnetic, and a descendant of Irish earls. Sharply conflicting traditions and ways of life doomed the Butler-Kemble union from the outset.

For the preceding fifty years, agitation in England against slavery and the slave trade had been constant, and Fanny Kemble had early absorbed British detestation of the hated institution. Butler had apparently told his wife nothing of his slave holdings before their marriage; she knew him only as a rich Philadelphian of private means. Revelation of the source of his income, therefore, came as a great shock to her. Writing in 1839, Kemble remarked, "When I married Mr. Butler I knew nothing of these dreadful possessions of his." Henceforth, from the moment that she learned the truth, she felt "a sense of horrible personal responsibility and implication . . . and I felt the weight of an unimagined guilt upon my conscience." In a letter to a friend in 1835 she wrote: "The family into which I married are large slaveholders; our present and future fortune depend greatly upon extensive plantations in Georgia. But the experience of every day, besides our faith in the great justice of God, forbids dependence on the duration of the mighty abuse by which one race of men is held in abject physical and mental slavery by another. As for me, though the toilsome earnings of my bread were to be my lot again tomorrow I should rejoice with unspeakable thankfulness that we had not to answer for what I consider so grievous a sin against humanity."

From this time on, Kemble was almost totally preoccupied with the slavery question, to the alarm and dismay of Pierce Butler and his family. She composed "a long and vehement treatise against Negro slavery" as part of her *Journal of a Residence in America,* an early work issued by a London publisher in 1835. Butler's angry opposition, however, caused her to delete this portion from the published book.

Actually, Kemble knew slavery only in the abstract. Her knowledge was based on extensive reading and her acquaintance with such dedicated antislavery advocates as William Ellery Channing, the eminent Boston Unitarian minister, and longtime friends Catharine Maria Sedgwick and her husband, Charles. Firsthand observation of slavery, Kemble determined, was essential to either confirm or to deny Pierce Butler's apologetics for—and the abolitionist's condemnation of—the institution. Nothing would satisfy but that she should visit her husband's plantation.

More than two years passed before Butler surrendered to his

wife's entreaties that she be allowed to accompany him on his next trip south. The long and arduous journey from Philadelphia to Butler Island, Georgia, began in December 1838. The details of the nine days' exhausting trek by railroad, stagecoach, and steamboat fill two chapters of Kemble's *Journal*. The primitive state of travel in America a century and a half ago is almost inconceivable today. The Butlers were accompanied on their strenuous expedition by their two infant daughters, Sarah and Frances, and an Irish nursemaid.

Kemble had resolved before undertaking the stay in Georgia that she would attempt to maintain an objective view. "I am going to Georgia," she wrote, "prejudiced against slavery, for I am an Englishwoman, in whom the absence of such a prejudice would be disgraceful." Nevertheless, she hoped to find mitigating factors in "the general injustice and cruelty of the system, perhaps much contentment on the part of the slaves and kindness on that of the masters." Accordingly, her report was to be based on careful observation and accurate facts, avoiding malice and noting any extenuating circumstances. Here could be tested Pierce Butler's claim that "those people are happy—happier than they would be if they were free. They love us and we are fond of them."

As soon as she arrived in Georgia, Kemble began writing her *Journal,* pouring into it her daily experiences and impressions, character sketches, descriptions of the surrounding area, and opinions on slavery. The period covered is from when the family left Philadelphia until April 17, 1839, when the Butlers returned North, a span of approximately four months.

The Butler estate consisted of two plantations. Dominant at the time was Butler Island, swampland devoted to the production of rice, which had become a highly profitable crop. The second plantation, Hampton Point on St. Simon's Island, was located on higher ground and had earlier been the center of the Butler property. The growing of sea-island cotton, however, had gradually exhausted the land, and by the time of Fanny Kemble's visit, pines and oaks were taking over the abandoned soil. At first, the Butlers stayed on Butler Island, but as the weather in the swamplands grew warmer and the danger of malaria increased, they moved to Hampton Point. Kemble's *Journal* is about equally divided between the two locations.

The *Journal* is made up of thirty-one letters, each addressed to "Dear Elizabeth." Although never written or mailed as letters, they were intended eventually to be read by Fanny's close friend, Elizabeth Dwight Sedgwick. When the *Journal* was published years later, it was dedicated to Elizabeth.

Contrary to the romantic notion that the owners of southern plantations lived in palatial mansions, nowhere on the Butler properties was there a civilized dwelling for Kemble and her family. On Butler Island, they moved into the overseer's shabby five-room cottage, and while there lived under the most primitive conditions. She describes the island itself as "a kind of mud sponge." She adds, "The chief produce of this delectable spot is rice—oranges, negroes, fleas, mosquitoes, various beautiful evergreens, sundry sort of snakes, alligators, and bull rushes enough to have made cradles not for Moses alone but the whole Israelitish host besides." The entire island lay below high-water mark, walled in by dikes; water from the Altamaha River was allowed in through ditches and canals when the rice fields needed flooding. Cabbages were the only vegetable grown on the island. There were three mills for threshing rice, run by steam and tidewater, and four slave villages where several hundred blacks were housed in wooden shacks.

The realities of the slave system exceeded Kemble's worst fears. Her *Journal,* which her great-granddaughter, Fanny Kemble Wister, claimed "is the only firsthand account by the wife of a slave holder of the negroes' lives on a plantation," is a day-by-day record of what she saw and did. She immediately gained the confidence of the black women, and they, hoping for her intercession on their behalf, told harrowing stories of the stripping and flogging of slave women, of hard manual labor being forced on women within three weeks after giving birth, of families being divided by the sale of slaves, and of women being forced to submit to the lusts of owners and overseers.

Most repulsive to Kemble was the lack of sanitation and general uncleanliness that pervaded everything. Her house servants, for example, were "perfectly filthy in their persons and clothes—

their faces, hands, and naked feet being literally incrusted with dirt." But, she pointed out, "this very disagreeable peculiarity does not prevent Southern women from hanging their infants at the breasts of Negresses, nor almost every planter's wife and daughter from having one or more little black pets sleeping like puppy dogs in their very bedchamber, nor almost every planter from admitting one or several of his female slaves to the still closer intimacy of his bed." Slavery, Kemble was convinced, was responsible for all such evils, "from lying, thieving, and adultery, to dirty houses, ragged clothes, and foul smells," because the system led inevitably to a total absence of self-respect.

Kemble's attempts to plead the causes of slaves that she believed to have been seriously mistreated, or to reform some of the worst aspects of slavery, were heard with impatience and resentment on the part of Pierce Butler, who made a few minor concessions in the beginning and then ordered her to bring no further complaints to him. His attitude was that nothing the slave women told his wife could be believed. "Why do you listen to such stuff?" he exclaimed angrily, "don't you know the niggers are all damned liars?" Kemble's sympathy for the slaves, in Butler's view, only tended to make them discontented and idle, neglectful of their work, and therefore more liable to punishment.

Thus began the estrangement between Pierce Butler and his wife, her loss of respect for him, and later their separation and divorce.

The degrading effects of slavery on southern whites deeply distressed Kemble. At the lowest social level were the poor who possessed no land or slaves. These "pinelanders" preferred a life of barbaric sloth and semistarvation to "working like niggers." To Kemble, "these wretched creatures" seemed hardly human, living in rude shelters, squatting on other men's land, and subsisting on wild fowl, venison and produce stolen from plantation gardens. In the eyes of the poor whites, physical labor was the portion of blacks and slaves alone.

The effect of slavery on the characters of the white masters was more subtle. From a superficial point of view, Kemble pointed out, "the habit of command gives them a certain self-possession and the enjoyment of leisure a certain ease." On closer acquaintance, however, the social system to which the slave owners belonged had infected them with less pleasing traits: "haughty, overbearing irritability, effeminate indolence, reckless extravagance, and a union of profligacy and cruelty, which are the immediate result of their irresponsible power over their dependents."

In considering the condition of the people on the Butler plantations as a whole, Kemble concluded that the principal physical hardships fell on women. Because slave women could gain their masters' favor by presenting them with a number of future slaves, some became mothers at the age of thirteen or fourteen. However, infant mortality was so high that no more than one out of two or three black babies could be expected to grow into an able-bodied adult worker. Because of the endless bending and lifting involved in their work, Kemble learned that many slave mothers lost more than one-half of their babies through miscarriages or stillbirths. The bodies of slave women were likely to be completely broken after twelve or fifteen births.

After the Butlers' stay in Georgia ended in April 1839, they returned to Philadelphia. Kemble had anticipated a second visit to the slave plantations, but her return was absolutely forbidden by John Butler, her husband's older brother. She therefore never saw the sea islands again.

Kemble began to give serious consideration to publication of her *Journal.* In 1840 she wrote to an intimate friend, Harriet St. Leger, "I have sometimes been haunted with the idea that it was an imperative duty, knowing what I know, and having seen what I have seen, to do all that lies in my power to show the dangers of this frightful institution." Pierce Butler was adamantly opposed to having any part of the document appear in print, and Kemble realized that to proceed against his wishes would mean the end of their marriage, already in a state of disintegration. The divorce came in 1849, but she continued to withhold her manuscript from publication. It was circulated privately, however, among friends in America and England. Meanwhile, the Butler estate in Georgia ceased to exist. The slaves were sold to pay Pierce Butler's debts incurred through reckless stock-market speculations and gambling.

Not until the outbreak of the Civil War did Kemble turn her

manuscript over to the British publisher, Longmans, who issued it in May 1863. A New York edition, published by Harper, appeared in July.

Before her trip south, Kemble had returned to England in October 1836 with her daughter, Sarah, and nurse. She remained for ten months. Pierce Butler joined her, but stayed only three weeks, after which the family came back to America. A second return to England came in late 1840, and the Pierce Butlers stayed in London for three years. They came back to Philadelphia in May 1843, but by that time, estrangement between them was complete. In November 1845, Kemble sailed alone for England, Butler refusing to give her custody of their two daughters.

After the Butlers' divorce in 1849, Kemble turned to a new career—public readings from Shakespeare's plays, immensely popular performances in America and England that she continued until age sixty-five. Her last years, until her death in 1893 at age eighty-four, were spent in London.

The *Journal of a Residence on a Georgian Plantation* lacks the romantic atmosphere of *Uncle Tom's Cabin.* It is missing the aristocratic characters, opulent mansions, and beautiful country estates that fascinated the readers of Harriet Beecher Stowe's best-selling novel. Kemble herself explained that her experience had been limited, and that life on a remote sea island should not be taken as typical of slave plantations everywhere in the South. Her observations were based on a stay of less than four months on two small islands at the mouth of the Altamaha River, an area about sixteen miles square but in the center of one of the South's most productive cotton, rice, and sugar areas.

It is probably an exaggeration to state, as did one writer (probably John Anthony Scott), that the *Journal* "more than any other book except *Uncle Tom's Cabin* helped to smash the old South, and wipe the plantation civilization out of existence." Readers in general, however, recognized the *Journal* as a dreadful indictment of slavery as an institution. The *London Review* conceded that it would have required the imagination of Dante to have conjured such a vision out of thin air. As the wife of a slavemaster, Kemble had reason to look for the best side of the system, and had hoped before going to Georgia to find ameliorating factors in it. Her inside story, from the point of view of a cultured Englishwoman, is unique in the annals of slavery. It fills a place occupied by no other writer in the history of the "peculiar institution." The historical and literary value of the *Journal* is therefore incontrovertible.

11. *A Retrospect of Western Travel*

Probably the most prolific and versatile woman writer of her time was Harriet Martineau, born in Norwich, England, the daughter of a cloth manufacturer. Her family's dire economic circumstances forced her to turn first to needlework and then to writing for self-support. She was further handicapped by complete deafness and the loss of her senses of smell and taste.

Before coming to America in 1834, ostensibly for health reasons, Martineau had established a considerable reputation in England for her religious stories and essays, some of which were widely circulated. Even more successful was a series of tales to illustrate the principles of political economy, written in language to appeal to common people. Her inspiration had been Adam Smith and other economists of the time.

With her fame fully recognized back in England, Martineau received a celebrity's reception in August 1834 when she landed in New York. Most educated Americans were familiar with her writings, and at first she was hospitably received as she began a two-year stay.

Before coming to the United States Martineau had already written against slavery, and she made no effort to conceal her hostility to the slave system. On the other hand, she announced that the purpose of her visit was not to write a book, that she had come without preconceived notions; her aim instead was to see as much as she could of the United States and to talk freely with people in all walks of life. Because of her deafness, she carried two kinds of ear trumpets and also had brought along a young companion, Louisa Jeffrey, to supplement her own observations. Some critics commented that Martineau had two serious handicaps other than physical problems—her enormous self-satisfaction, which convinced her of the rightness of all her conclusions, and her excessive garrulity.

In the course of her two-year sojourn, Martineau managed to cover practically all accessible regions of the new nation. Her travels extended as far west as Mackinac and Chicago, and as far south as New Orleans. During her first winter, she made a tour in the South, where she was hospitably received. Transportation facilities, however, were primitive, with few miles of local railroads, while stage coaches had to contend with nearly impassible roads. Southern wayside inns were even worse. At one stop, Martineau was served an unidentified dish. "According to some," she reported, "it was mutton; to others pork; my own idea is that it was dog."

From New York, she went up the Hudson to Albany and, of course, to Niagara. Enduring friendships were formed with Ralph Waldo Emerson and William Lloyd Garrison. At an abolitionist mass meeting in Boston, Martineau was outspoken in expressing her antislavery sentiments. Thereafter, she met with much prejudice and suffered many slights and insults. The southern press denounced her as a dangerous incendiary. During further journeys, she was received coldly by the respectable people. In fact, threats of personal injury forced Martineau to abandon a journey down the Ohio, and she was threatened again during a tour to the northern lakes. These experiences naturally confirmed her abolitionist views.

The scope of Martineau's travels, especially considering the difficulties of the era's primitive transportation, was amazing. In New Jersey, she saw the cotton factories and Passaic Falls; she then went on to Pittsburgh and over the Alleghenies, spent six weeks in Philadelphia, three weeks in Baltimore, and five weeks in Washington. In the capital, she enjoyed the hospitality of President Andrew Jackson and several department heads, became acquainted with most prominent senators (including Henry Clay, Calhoun, and Webster), and was on friendly terms with Judge Story and other Supreme Court justices. Her next stop was "Jefferson's University" in Charlottesville, where she was the first

British visitor to be entertained. From that point, Martineau went on to Richmond, where the Virginia legislature was in session, undertook a "long wintry journey" through North and South Carolina to Charleston, went on to New Orleans, up the Mississippi and Ohio to Cincinnati and Nashville, and finally back to New York. Before she returned to England in August 1836, her last expedition was to Detroit by way of Lake Erie, across the state of Michigan, around to Chicago, and back through Ohio and Pennsylvania.

Back in England, Martineau was besieged with offers from London publishers for her impressions of America. Even though her original intention was not to write such an account, she proceeded to produce two three-volume works. The first, *Society in America,* was planned as a systematic examination of just how the Americans were applying the principles of the Constitution and the Declaration of Independence. The second, of more interest to general readers, *A Retrospect of Western Travel,* records incidents of travel, impressions of distinguished persons, and descriptions of people and places.

During the course of her long stay in the southern states, almost everything that she saw was repugnant to Martineau. She found that slavery was degrading to both master and slave. The ruling class was corrupted by its belief that labor was disgraceful, and the wives of slaveholders were "as much slaves as their Negroes." At complete variance with the Declaration, which proclaimed that all men are "born free and equal," was the institution of slavery itself.

Next to their treatment of blacks, Martineau objected to the Americans' attitude toward women. In her opinion, the voteless condition of women could hardly be reconciled with the principle that government derives its just powers from the consent of the governed. Women were not treated equally in education, and they were discouraged from expressing their opinions or in exercising freedom of the mind. The opportunities for female employment were few, and virtually the only career open to women was marriage.

Despite her strictures on America, Martineau believed that most of the faults she described were temporary stumbling blocks and would be corrected in time. She concludes:

The striking effect upon a stranger of witnessing, for the first time, the absence of poverty, of gross ignorance, of all servility, of all insolence of manner, cannot be exaggerated in description. I have seen every man in the towns an independent citizen; every man in the country a land-owner. I had seen that the villagers had their newspapers, the factory girls their libraries. I had witnessed the controversies between candidates for office on some difficult subjects, of which the people were to be the judges.

In her *Autobiography,* however, published in 1877, long after her American experiences, Martineau expressed sharp criticisms omitted from her earlier works. She ridiculed the strange management of children proposed by Bronson Alcott of Concord; the inordinate ambition, insincerity, and double-dealing of such politicians as Webster, Clay, and Calhoun; and the indifference of northern intellectuals such as Margaret Fuller to the antislavery movement. She also regarded the aftermath of the Civil War as deeply disappointing. Her last recorded comment on America was "I am, like many others, almost in despair for the Great Republic."

Although her abolitionist opinions and unflattering comments were resented by some Americans, Harriet Martineau ranks with Frances Trollope as one of the most widely read, popular, and influential English women travelers in nineteenth-century America.

12. *A Diary in America, with Remarks on Its Institutions*

When Captain Frederick Marryat visited the United States in 1837, he was famous as the author of *Peter Simple, Midshipman Easy,* and other sea stories. He had fought in many naval battles during the last years of the Napoleonic wars, rising to the rank of captain in the Royal Navy. He resigned his commission in 1830 to devote all his time to writing.

Marryat had an inbred suspicion of democracy, and it is apparent that a principal purpose of his American tour was to discredit democratic institutions.

His intention to visit America had been stated in 1836, when he wrote: "Do the faults of this people (to wit, the Swiss) arise from the peculiarity of their constitutions, or from the nature of their government? To ascertain this, one must compare them with those who live under similar institutions. I must go to America—that's decided."

The timing of Marryat's visit was unfortunate to some degree. When he landed in New York City on May 4, 1837, the country was in the midst of one of the most severe depressions it had ever experienced. People were too occupied with closing banks and with mass unemployment to pay much attention to the visiting novelist. Nevertheless, Marryat was well received in New York City, dined with the best people, and capitalized upon his reputation.

Although the announced motive of Marryat's visit was to make a study of comparative government and of the effects of democracy on a people, he also wanted to gather new material for his writings; travel literature was both popular and financially rewarding. To gather his facts, he toured the country over a period of eighteen months. For various reasons, he was unable to travel as extensively as he had hoped—never getting into the Deep South, for example—but he did manage to cover much ground.

Marryat remained in New York until July, except for three short excursions to Boston, to Passaic Falls in New Jersey, and up the Hudson to West Point. He was a guest of Mayor Aaron Hill at a public dinner, where he listened uncomfortably to spread-eagle oratory accompanying a Fourth of July celebration. Shortly afterward, he left New York to begin the first part of his continental swing. He traveled north by steamboat up the Hudson to Albany, where he visited the Albany Female Academy and then made a short detour to Niskayuna, a Shaker settlement near Albany, where he witnessed with disgust a Shaker meeting that he characterized to be the "degradation of rational and immortal beings."

Marryat was tremendously impressed by Niagara Falls, which he reached by train, canal boat, and steamer. From Niagara, he went on to Buffalo, Detroit, and Mackinac. At Mackinac, he met the Indian agent on the island, Henry R. Schoolcraft, whose opinion of the visitor was generally unfavorable: "Anything but a quiet, modest, English gentleman." After stopovers in Toronto and Montreal, Marryat turned south to visit Philadelphia, a city whose well-kept streets and houses charmed him. In Washington he was unsuccessful in persuading Congress to revise the American copyright law, which gave no protection to works published outside the United States. However he approved of President Van Buren, whom he described to be "a very gentleman-like man" who had dared, unlike Andrew Jackson, to prevent "the mobocracy from intruding themselves at his levees."

After a return trip to Canada and Mackinac, Marryat proceeded on to the Wisconsin territory and from there down the Mississippi to St. Louis, then up the Ohio River to Louisville and Cincinnati. The tour concluded with brief visits to Virginia

Springs and Lexington, Kentucky. He left New York for England at the end of November.

The editor of one edition of Marryat's *Diary in America,* Jules Zangen, comments "of all the literary lions who have made their progress through the drawing-rooms and the backwoods of America, laying up treasures for the inevitable 'authoritative account,' perhaps the most tactless and blundering was Captain Frederick Marryat." When he arrived in 1837, he was received as an honored guest, but before his American visit was completed he had been threatened by a lynch mob, had watched his books burned in public bonfires, and at least twice had seen himself hung in effigy by angry crowds. Major Philip Hone of New York wrote, "It would have been better for both parties if the sailor-author had been known on this side of the Atlantic only by his writings."

Why this outburst of American outrage and resentment? It was triggered by a toast Marryat offered at a dinner in Toronto, where he was a guest. Marryat's toast was "To Captain Drew and his brave comrades, who cut out the *Caroline.*" The *Caroline* had been an American vessel engaged in carrying guns, supplies, and volunteers to the Canadian rebels entrenched on Navy Island in the Niagara River, just above Niagara Falls. British boats under the command of Lieutenant Drew crossed the river to the American side where the *Caroline* was anchored, boarded her, set her afire, and tried to push her over the Falls. The American press soon afterward was filled with indignant editorials condemning the attack. Marryat's tactless toast involved him in the controversy, and he was widely damned for being an ungrateful wretch who had accepted American hospitality and then betrayed it.

Marryat crossed swords with the American press on another occasion. While visiting in Louisville, he became romantically involved with a doctor's wife. The newspapers had a field day over the affair. The Captain contributed a long letter to the *Louisville Journal,* complaining bitterly of his treatment by the press.

Immediately after his return to England, Marryat published his *A Diary in America, with Remarks on Its Institutions* in two series of three volumes each. The work was reprinted in Philadelphia by Carey and Hart, who were generous enough to pay the author $2,250 for it and a novel.

In the *Diary,* Marryat commented favorably on the American character, especially its energy and enterprise. He had no liking for the American government, however, asserting that it was not a republican government at all, but a democracy, by which he meant that it was a "mob government," with a popular majority in direct control instead of elected wise representatives.

The *Diary* is a travelogue. Marryat recorded faithfully much that he saw, although he often added superficial generalizations based on poor evidence. Indicative of the contemporary interest in the picturesque and romantic, there are many descriptions of rivers, waterfalls, and lakes, and about 10 percent of the total text is devoted to Indians.

When Marryat wrote about American political institutions, the stated reason for his visit, his Tory views were much in evidence. Beginning with the election of Andrew Jackson in 1828, he charged, the American government had become too democratic, leaving the mob in charge. According to Marryat, Jackson and his friends had "destroyed the moral courage of the American people, and without moral courage what chance is there of any fixed standards of morality?" Ruin was the inevitable result of bad government.

Marryat was convinced that the principle of equality was evil and the best government was a benevolent aristocracy born to govern. Mob [i.e., majority] rule would turn liberty into license. Society, in his view, was like a naval vessel, where the officers were the ruling class and the seamen were the people. Each had its proper position and duties. America's political, social, and moral future was endangered unless a conservative aristocracy could be created and take power.

Marryat generally avoided the subject of slavery, although he discussed the plight of the free black in the North, whose condition he found appalling. He was sharply critical, too, of the government's many breaches of faith with the Indians and the effects of the white man's civilization on Indian culture.

Marryat devotes a considerable amount of space to correcting what he conceived as errors in the writings of other travelers. He ridicules Frances Trollope. He is even more critical of Harriet Martineau for her many "absurdities and fallacies," to the point of accusing her of telling falsehoods, perhaps because her political views were diometrically opposed to his own.

Americans' reaction to *A Diary in America* was largely unfavorable when it appeared in 1839. Typical was an opinion expressed by George Templeton Strong, the New York social historian: "Mrs. Trollope can't hold a candle to the captain in fertility of invention. He don't lie like a gentleman, either . . . but rampages in his mendacity like any loafer."

Among American reviewers, neither *Godey's* nor the *Ladies Companion* found any merit in the book. The *New York Review* was kinder, pointing out that "perhaps the greatest merit of the book is that it is very entertaining . . . many personal adventures are related in a jovial and good natured style, and containing apt and vigorous illustrations of his graver matter."

Marryat was not a political philosopher, and his book is not the authoritative work on the weaknesses and failings of democracy in America that he had planned to write. It is doubtful that his caustic comments either helped or harmed the cause of conservatism in America or Britain. Yet Marryat was a shrewd observer, and his descriptions are filled with a wealth of detail. He had a keen reporter's eye, and the glimpses that he recorded of people and places encountered during his travels are a valuable source of information about the everyday aspects of life in America in the 1830s. Marryat's novel-writing experience helped him to dramatize and enliven his accounts and avoid the humdrum nature and simply factual nature of most diaries.

13. *The Eastern and Western States of America*

Allan Nevins characterized James Silk Buckingham as "one of the most intelligent, energetic, and liberal of British visitors to America before the Civil War." Buckingham, the son of a retired English merchant, was sent as a child to the naval academy at Falmouth, and began his naval career at age nine. He saw active service in the naval wars with France and was a prisoner for a time when captured by a French corvette. He abandoned his naval career when he witnessed the harsh discipline to which common sailors were subjected. The sea appears to have been in his blood, however, for at age twenty-one he became captain of a West Indiaman and for some years made voyages to many parts of the world. Later, he served as a member of Parliament for Sheffield and established a reputation as an advocate of social reform. He also tried his hand at journalism by founding the *Athenaeum* in 1828.

Buckingham's travels in America were spread over a three-year period, 1837–40. His primary mission was to lecture on temperance and other reforms. It appears that he met with a warm reception from religious organizations and temperance societies. Buckingham was also an eloquent advocate of education, the betterment of the working class, free trade, and universal peace. It was estimated that his lectures were heard or read by at least a million Americans.

Like other English travelers of the time, Buckingham did not hesitate to call attention to faults that he found in American society. Among specific shortcomings pointed out by him: people were always in a hurry, they were over-sensitive to English criticism, they kept late hours, ate too fast, took insufficient exercise, had disgusting habits in the use of tobacco, and an avid appetite for quack medicines. A cynical yellow press had too much influence, and excessive violence prevailed, as shown by the murder rate. On the other hand, he commended American charitable and educational institutions and general spirit of liberalism.

Buckingham was a prolific author. He wrote no less than eight volumes on his American experiences and observations: *America, Historical, Statistic, and Descriptive* (1841, three volumes), *The Slave States of America* (1842, two volumes), and *The Eastern and Western States of America* (1842, three volumes). Because of its encyclopedic character, only selected items from the last title will be considered here.

From the outset, Buckingham expresses his adamant opposition to slavery. He quotes southern defenders of the system as claiming that slaves were better off than free blacks; on one hand they were comfortably cared for, on the other, the free black would be reduced to precarious want and misery. After observing free blacks in the North, Buckingham was convinced that they were much better off than their enslaved brethren in the South, despite strong prejudices they met among northerners.

Buckingham praised the inventiveness and ingenuity of Americans, some of the work of which he saw exhibited in a Mechanics Fair in New York. He cited such examples as a machine for splitting wood into shingles, one for making boxes, another for knitting stockings, and a variety of other useful items. It was noted that "In the making of arms, guns, pistols, and swords, the Americans excel." Also rated as superior were cabinetware in furniture, cut glass, bronze and silver work, and hardware. On a much larger scale, "some of the newest and finest of merchant ships" were being built in Boston, New York, Baltimore, and Philadelphia, believed by Buckingham ahead of "all other nations of the world."

Because education was a matter of great concern to Buckingham, he investigated the status of schools and colleges wherever he went. Connecticut's educational system, in particular, met with his warm approval. There provision was made for schools at all levels, ranging from common schools for all children (about 90,000) up to academies, colleges, and theological seminaries, with Yale University at the top. At the time, Yale had the largest number of students (500) of any college in the country. Its curriculum included elocution, chemistry, law, theology, and medicine. "Teachers of modern languages were not reckoned members of the faculty." The Yale Library held more than 20,000 volumes.

During a visit to Cincinnati, Buckingham surveyed the educational situation in that city. He reported detailed facts about the College of Ohio for general collegiate education; a medical college; the Lane Seminary for theological studies; the Woodward Academy, a high school; the College of Professional Teachers, a normal school; and the Athenaeum, a large Catholic institution; 20 public schools, with 40 teachers and 2,500 pupils of both sexes; 28 private schools, with 600 pupils; and 9 infant schools, with about 300 pupils.

Buckingham is critical of the "demoralized state" of the American press. He conceded that there were "able, honorable, and moral editors," but also "unprincipled and profligate ones." The latter he blamed on "the morbid appetite of the public for scandal, obscenity, and attacks on private character." Buckingham was especially vehement in his denunciation of the *New York Morning Herald*, "which has more obscenity, irreligion, and private slander in it than is to be found in all the papers of the State besides, has an immense circulation in all classes."

The frequency of marriage between girls sixteen to eighteen years of age to men of fifty and sixty was viewed doubtfully by Buckingham. The girls often had been brought up with expensive tastes, living beyond their means, and they and their mothers were therefore on the lookout for an older man, bachelor or widower, who could indulge their extravagant habits with his good income.

The state of religion in America received much attention from Buckingham. In every city or community visited, he counted the number of churches and denominations represented. He offers a graphic description of a Methodist revival in Carlisle, Pennsylvania, which occurred during his visit there. The activity went on in a crowded church from sunset to midnight for fifteen nights in succession, without an intermission. Buckingham reported that he felt "a compound of surprise, awe, sorrow, pity, and terror. It was like being in an assembly of maniacs." He was convinced that more orderly religious worship was productive of more permanent benefit.

In Germantown, Pennsylvania, Buckingham witnessed a Presbyterian revival that went on night and day for three weeks. The chief features were "excitement, passionate exclamation, vehement praying, moaning, and lamentation." Other churches in the village were having meetings of a similar nature, but marked by "less violent emotions."

Later, during his stay in Philadelphia, Buckingham noted that religious excitement often prevailed along with political excitement. In fact, he concluded, "Excitement of some kind or other seems indispensable to the existence of an American," both men and women.

Buckingham wondered about the want "of confidence in, and respect for, the ruling authorities, so general in America." His conclusions were that there were six principal causes for the popular attitude: insufficient parental discipline, young men with too much money, need for feminine influence to soften extreme political agitation, too free use of tobacco and alcohol, overimpatience to become wealthy, and, in the South especially, the influence of the slave system, which trained young minds to tyrannize over others.

Like most European visitors, Buckingham was disgusted with Americans' use of tobacco. During Buckingham's call on the president of Transylvania University in Lexington, Kentucky, the venerable gentleman smoked a cigar and "chewed copiously" at the same time. Boys of ten or twelve had their own quids and cigars. The fumes of this "nauseous and filthy weed were so offensive to females," according to Buckingham, "that all smoking is prohibited in stage-coaches, railroads, steamboats, and apartments in hotels in which ladies are seated." He also blamed the tobacco habit for exciting thirst for such alcoholic stimulants as mint juleps, brandy, and cold punches.

Perhaps inspired by Robert Owen's experiments at New Harmony, Indiana, Buckingham found the concept of communitarian or cooperative communities of special interest. He investigated, visited, and reported on attempts to establish such groups in the United States, especially the Rappites in Pennsylvania and New Harmony, and considered the reasons for their failure despite idealistic founders.

Buckingham described the fate of wild life in America: "There are no longer any wild animals in the State of Ohio." A half century earlier, buffalo, elk, bear, panther, and fox had been numerous, but by the time of Buckingham's visit, the larger animals had disappeared almost entirely, leaving only the opossum, raccoon, fox, polecat, mink, squirrel, groundhog, and rabbit. Beavers were gone, but a few otters still remained. Rattlesnakes and several other species of snakes were common.

Buckingham visited many cities and towns beyond the East Coast and in the Midwest and describes the principal features of Pittsburgh, Cincinnati, Lexington, Chillicothe, Dayton, and other communities. Pittsburgh was "certainly the most smoky and sooty town it has ever yet been my lot to behold." In Cincinnati, he saw "Mrs. Trollope's Folly," which he called "a grotesque combination of Gothic, Greek, Egyptian, and Norman architecture." At Watervleite, a visit was made to a Shaker village, which Buckingham called a "superstitious and deluded community." The number of members was declining because of the Shaker prohibition against marriage.

In Buckingham's view, there were striking differences between the adjoining slave state of Kentucky and the free state of Ohio. In Kentucky, most of the laborers were slaves "indifferent to everything but their own ease and their desire to escape from labor, slovenliness and dirtiness were predominant." By contrast, in Ohio, where a majority of laborers were white, "neatness, order, and cleanliness are remarkable in all their villages, cottages, and farms."

Buckingham ends the second volume of his travels with an impassioned plea for temperance and a condemnation of the evils of strong drink—a prime purpose of his American mission and the subject of many lectures.

In his third and last volume, Buckingham returns to the Northeast, and devotes some 500 pages to a detailed account of his stay in upstate New York—primarily Buffalo, Rochester, Auburn, Syracuse, and Utica—and then Vermont, New Hampshire, and Massachusetts. Many chapters deal with virtually every aspect of life in Boston: early history, educational system, religious establishments, business and industry, press, politics and government, prisons, population, and much more. Several weeks in November and December 1840 were spent in Providence, Fall River, New Bedford, and Plymouth, before Buckingham sailed from New York at the end of December to return to England.

In a second series, Buckingham described extensive travels through other regions of the country: the southern and midwestern areas, as far south as New Orleans and north to Toronto, Montreal, and Quebec.

Buckingham's eight volumes on his three years in America are detailed and full of facts. His total impression, based on his widespread journeys, is generally favorable. If the country could continue to be wisely governed, and not be weakened by luxury, intemperance, and war, he concluded, there were no real limits to its future greatness.

William Oliver (n.d.)

14. *Eight Months in Illinois, with Information to Emigrants*

As the number of immigrants, travelers, and other visitors to America steadily increased after the Revolution, there was an almost insatiable demand for firsthand accounts of what new-comers might expect to find in their new homes. A popular form of travel literature was guides for immigrants. Random examples worthy of mention are William Amphlett's *The Emigrant's Directory to the Western States of North America* (1819); John Knight's *The Emigrant's Best Instructor* (1818); William Cobbett's *The Emigrant's Guide* (1830); S. H. Collins's *The Emigrant's Guide to and Description of the United States* (1830); Joseph Pickering's *Enquiries of an Emigrant* (1832); J. Regan's *Emigrants Guide to the Western States of America* (1832); and W. Hancock's *An Emigrant's Five Years in the Free States of America* (1860).

Writing about one such work, William Oliver's *Eight Months in Illinois, with Information to Emigrants,* the historian Max Berger declared: "As a document on the economic history of the Mid-west, this little book has few equals. As regards crops, farming meth-ods, and the rural folkways of the period, the work is unexcelled."

Oliver came to Illinois as an English immigrant in 1841. The author's announced purpose was to meet the needs of the "poorer classes" by providing as much information as was practicable as inexpensively as possible, rather than adding to the numerous popular books about American travel already available.

Oliver entered the United States by way of London and New York, proceeding on by steamboat in early December to Philadelphia and Harrisburg, across the Alleghenies to Pittsburgh, Cincinnati, and Louisville to the Mississippi River. Turning north toward Illinois, he stopped at Chester, Kaskaskia, Plum Prairie, and Flat Prairie.

The population of Randolph County, Illinois, Oliver's first destination, was international in character—Dutch, German, Swiss, Irish, Scotch, and a few English. There were former slaveholders from southern states, disillusioned with the slavery system. The leading religious denominations were well represented. In order of size there were: Methodist, Baptist, Presbyterian, Congregational, Campbellite, United Brethren, Dunkards, Lutheran, Protestant Episcopal, Quaker or Friends, and Catholic.

Oliver found an unexpected degree of superstition or belief in witchcraft, omens, and luck prevalent among the people, especially hunters, many of whom could not read or write.

Neighbors gathered to husk huge quantities of corn for the preparation of bread and other bakery goods, to drink alcoholic beverages (if they were permitted), to play at dances, and to observe the hog-killing season around Christmas and New Year. Hogs in Illinois at the time were described as thin, long-nosed, speedy, agile creatures, with legs like greyhounds'.

Oliver reported that pioneer frontiersmen or woodchoppers took pride in their prowess. With practice, they could bring down large trees with comparative ease and learn the technique of rail splitting. A chopping bee, numbering twenty or thirty men, was a very animated affair.

Every person or domestic animal on the farm relied on the main crop, corn, in one form or another; stalks, leaves, and husks were used as fodder for cattle and horses. Ranking below corn but high in total acreage in Illinois were various other crops: wheat, oats, uplands rice, barley, cotton, tobacco, potatoes (white and sweet), melons, pumpkins, and turnips. Hay could be grown in quantity on the prairie.

Illinois cattle were a mixed breed, a combination of many European varieties. The cows were not fed enough to keep them growing or healthy or to save the calves during long winters. Cattle diseases such as "hollow horn" and "white evil" were a menace to animals as well as humans.

The rearing of horses was a profitable business in Oliver's time. There was a ready market, and the expense of raising them was trifling.

Oliver believed that some sound investments were essential for businessmen: well-stocked general stores, grist mills, good saw mills, and wind mills if they were not to be located in too stormy an area.

Oliver offers a number of comments on the state of education in Illinois, citing the provisions for the support of public education voted by the U.S. Congress such as land for the use of schools. His chief criticisms of the existing system were the unqualified teachers needing examiners to test their competence and the poor financial rewards received by the teaching profession.

Good physicians were rare in the Illinois country, and there were many unprincipled quacks practicing. Calomel was the universal remedy for any ailment.

Oliver dwelt at length on the future of American game animals. Even at that early date, a century and a half ago, it was evident that some species were vanishing. The bison were being slaughtered for the sake of their skins at the rate of 150,000 to 200,000 annually. Elk and deer were scarce. Other animals whose numbers were declining were wolves, bears, cougars, beavers, skunks, minks, foxes, wild turkeys, quails, prairie chickens, and horned owls. Insects, however, appeared in armies: mosquitoes, house flies, ants, cockroaches, ticks, and other pests all tormented the traveler.

Nature was no less generous with serpent life, as reported by Oliver, although they generally were harmless. Poisonous rattlesnakes were outnumbered twenty to one by other snakes. Copperheads and yellow mocassins were plentiful and dangerous, however some of the Indians' remedies were fairly effective for their bites.

By mid-September 1842, Oliver was ready to begin his return voyage to England. After leaving Illinois, he and a partner made stops in principal cities all the way back to New York. During the eight months of his journey, most cities had expanded since he had first seen them.

The primary purpose of Oliver's trip was to obtain information on the basis of which he could advise immigrants about the desirability of acquiring land and settling in Illinois or elsewhere in the Midwest. After reviewing the many factors discussed in his *Eight Months in Illinois,* he attempts to be noncommittal and reasonably objective.

> I wish it to be distinctly understood that I advise no man, whatever may be his circumstances, to emigrate, either to Illinois or to any other part of the world. I have arranged the information I possess, and have laid it before those who think of emigrating, that they may have the materials for forming a judgment for themselves. But whilst I am unwilling to advise, I may perhaps be allowed to give a caution. Let no one whose prospects are good at home rashly think of emigrating. The poor, those who see unavoidable difficulty approaching them, and such as have families without any adequate provision for them, are the proper immigrants to a new country, where thews and sinews are commutible into wealth; and to such many parts of the United States will afford a fitting and welcome asylum. Still it is a new country, a country of strangers, and of new habits, which form a complete and often not very pleasing contrast to those already acquired; and *home* is the word universally used by emigrants, when speaking of their native land. Neither do I wish to recommend any particular state in the Union, for although there are places which I prefer to others, still there are advantages and disadvantages in all. I have written chiefly about Illinois, because I happen to know more about it than the rest of the states.

15. *Civilization in the United States*

Matthew Arnold's writings on America began before he ever crossed the Atlantic to verify his opinions. When he was sixty, he decided to go to the United States on a lecture tour for several reasons: to confirm views he had already expressed, to help improve American culture, and to reap the substantial financial rewards that would come to a famous English author. Americans knew Arnold as the son of Dr. Thomas Arnold of Rugby, and as a distinguished poet, a former Oxford University professor, and the author of many books.

Arnold spent a half year in America, from October 1883 to March 1884. Although he drew large audiences in most cities, his lectures came close to being disasters. His voice was too weak to project, was monotonous, his English accent confused listeners, and he read his lectures from manuscript. The problems were solved when, on the advice of friends, he took voice lessons from an elocutionist.

Neither was Arnold's personality ingratiating. In the sharp judgment of a Chicago newspaper, "He has harsh features, supercilious manners, parts his hair down the middle, wears a single eyeglass, and ill-fitting clothes." A more sympathetic critic, Charles Norton, agreed that "Arnold's delivery is not good, but is striking from its thorough Anglican seriousness and awkwardness. It does not hurt the substance of his lectures, or their effect on the audience. Indeed the common hearer seems to be impressed by the fact that it is the matter not the manner of his speech that is of primary consequence."

There is little of a typical travelogue about Arnold's account of his stay in the United States. His concern was primarily with social and political matters, on which he had firm views. In 1885, he published *Discourses in America*. Three years later, in the year of his death, his *Civilization in the United States* appeared, consisting of four parts: the title essay, "A Word About America," "A Word More About America," and "General Grant." In the last, he expressed great admiration for Grant's simple and sterling character.

At the outset, Arnold comments that American institutions were well adapted to solving political and social problems and flexible in dealing with changing circumstances and conditions. Because it was relatively free of class distinctions, he felt that the American population tended to be homogeneous, with less division between rich and poor. Yet to a wealthy, cultured Englishman, for example, such a society had shortcomings. For "the great bulk of the community . . . things in America are favorable. It is easier for them there than in the Old World to rise and make their fortune . . . society seems organized there for their benefit." The key word for Arnold in judging a civilization is *interesting,* meaning having distinction and beauty—elements he found lacking in America because of monotonous landscapes, ugly place names, and shoddy architecture. The American passion for democracy glorified the average individual, the yellow press vulgarized everything it touched, and defects were covered up by bragging.

Some of Arnold's sharpest criticisms were aimed at American newspapers:

> I should say that if one were searching for the best means to efface and kill in a whole nation the discipline of respect, the feeling for what is elevated, one could not do better than take the American newspapers. The absence of truth and soberness in them, the poverty in serious interest, the personality and sensation mongering are beyond belief. . . . In general, the daily papers are such that when one returns home one is moved to admiration and thankfulness not only at the great London papers, like the *Times* or the *Standard,* but quite as much at the great provincial papers, too.

Arnold concedes that a few newspapers were in whole, or in part, exceptions. The *New York Nation,* a weekly paper, was comparable in quality to the English *Saturday Review*, but it was edited by a foreigner and had a very limited sale.

Americans did not admit, however, that their newspapers were a scandal, and maintained that their press was top-notch. In the same way, instead of recognizing that America had produced little literature of importance, they pretended that for every English writer there was an American one to match. Thus, they read second-rate authors like Roe instead of Dickens and Scott. Arnold saw such self-glorification and self-deception as an American danger.

The root of the problem, at least in part Arnold felt, was that Americans were highly nervous, a state caused by worry, overwork, want of exercise, injudicious diet, and a most trying climate. The best hope for the country's salvation, Arnold declared, lay in the many cultivated, judicious, delightful individuals he met in the course of his travels. As matters stood when he was writing, "The *average man* is too much a religion there; his performance is unduly magnified, his shortcomings are not duly seen and admitted."

Arnold's conception of the American Revolution is at variance with the usual American and British interpretations: "The British rule which they threw off was not one of oppressors and tyrants which declaimers suppose, and the merit of the Americans was not that of oppressed men rising against tyrants, but rather of sensible young people getting rid of stupid and overweening guardians who misunderstood and mismanaged them."

Arnold was somewhat critical of the voices and intonations of American women, but added, "Almost every one acknowledges that there is a charm in American women—a charm which you find in almost all of them, wherever you go. It is the charm of a natural manner, a manner not self-conscious, artificial, and constrained," to a much greater extent than among English women. It was seen as one of the good effects of equality upon social life and manners.

Arnold argues that there is little basic difference between an Englishman and an American, especially in the beginning. He claims that "the Americans have produced plenty of men strong, shrewd, upright, able, effective; very few who are highly distinguished. Alexander Hamilton is indeed a man of rare distinction; Washington, though he has not the high mental distinction of Pericles or Caesar, has true distinction of style and character. But these men belong to the pre-American age . . . Washington is but an Englishman, an English officer. The typical American is Abraham Lincoln."

Arnold sums up his case by stating that what really dissatisfies in American civilization is want of being *interesting* that stems from the want of elevation and beauty. Any change would require stern self-criticism and willingness to recognize shortcomings in American culture and civilization. "To us," Arnold emphasizes, "the future of the United States is of incalculable importance. Already we feel their influence much, and we shall feel it more." Each has a great deal to learn from the other.

16. *The Western World*

It is generally conceded by historians that Alexander Mackay was the most penetrating and sympathetic foreign commentator on American institutions and political life before James Bryce.

Mackay was no fly-by-night superficial observer who wrote about the New World after a short tour. In fact, he was quite critical of such travel writers and was determined not to be one of them. A Scotsman, he had edited a newspaper in Toronto and then joined the staff of the *London Morning Chronicle,* for which he reported congressional debates on the Oregon question in 1846.

In preparation for writing *The Western World,* Mackay mapped out an extensive itinerary for 1846–47, making a circuit of the Union that included the South and Southwest, the Mississippi Valley, the Great Lakes, western Pennsylvania, western New York, and, of course, the seaboard states. His announced object was to "comprehend the social life of America, the working of its political institutions, and the bearing of its policy upon its moral development." For such a mission to succeed, he declared, "it is absolutely essential that a man should step aside from the hotel, the railway and the steamer, and live with the people, instead of living, as the mere traveler does, beside them."

Mackay was a convinced liberal, tolerant and understanding of the American way of life while recognizing its crudities and deficiencies. It is clear from his writings that he was persuaded of the superiority of the American political system over the British, as well as of many American ways and institutions.

Mackay devoted a considerable amount of space to analyzing the American character, in part to refute certain misconceptions spread by other travelers from abroad. For example, he did not find Americans gloomy and reserved as some had reported, but "if properly approached, they are frank, communicative, and not infrequently even mercurial in their dispositions." Mackay agreed that Americans were oversensitive, but blamed the fact on their feelings having been "wantonly and unnecessarily wounded by successive travelers," and by the young nation not yet being certain of its place in the world. A natural reaction to such uncertainty is a tendency toward boastfulness, a weakness often mentioned by foreign commentators. In Mackay's view, however, there were grounds for American pride. He noted, "there is no other country on earth which in so short a time has accomplished so much."

One manifestation of Americans' patriotism was confidence in their form of government; they were convinced that a democratic government best served their interests. Mackay emphasizes that "the American Republic differs essentially from all that have preceded it in the principles on which it was founded . . . it is a Democratic Republic, in the broadest sense of the term." Furthermore, the success and stability of such a form of government depend on an enlightened, educated people—an American ideal. Mackay found deep faith among Americans about the destiny of their country. At a time when the Union consisted of thirty states, they had no doubt that eventually the nation would embrace the entire continent.

Other features of American society Mackay observed included a fondness for titles (which he attributes to a natural desire for distinction); a love of money ("a weakness to which humanity must universally plead guilty"); an extraordinary talent for invention; a love of being well dressed as a sign of respectability; and employment for all able and willing hands—from all of which Mackay concluded that "America is the country for the industrious and hard-working man."

Commenting upon American education and letters, Mackay was impressed by the fact that nearly all persons that he met were able to read and write, in contrast to the "ignorant multitudes in other lands." He praised the rise of a national literature marked by the writings of Cooper, Halleck, Pierpont, Dana, Bryant, Irving, and Bancroft, and important contributions in the fields of medicine and law. Also noted were the prolific output of periodicals and newspapers; "the proportion of daily papers is enormous."

Mackay discussed the effects of the separation of church and state in America at length: "There is no principle more freely admitted, both practically and theoretically, in America than the right of every man to think for himself on all matters connected with religion." There was no evidence, he believed, that separation was harmful to the vitality and energy of religion in America. On the contrary, the number of churches, the extent and character of congregations, the frequency of meetings, the fervor of religious exercises, and the strong financial support proved that the voluntary principle was sound. Mackay took a dim view, however, of certain extreme, even fanatical, sects. He described a revival meeting where the preacher in the pulpit was "sometimes foaming at the mouth," weaker members of the congregation became hysterical, and hundreds were converted in a day. But once the excitement died down, backsliding was worse than before.

Political aspects of the United States fascinated Mackay. The basic principle upon which the system is based, he noted at the beginning, was the political equality of man. On that foundation was built "one of the most elaborate political devices on earth," and further, "the American constitution is one of the most ingenious pieces of political mechanism that ever resulted from the deliberations of man." A remarkable feature of the federal system, in Mackay's eyes, was the establishment of a single executive, the president, with vast powers. Separate chapters are devoted to the workings of the Congress, comparisons of the House and Senate, and to the judiciary system of the United States. Mackay also considered the relations between the federal and state governments.

In chapters titled "Slavery in Its Political Aspect" and "Slavery in Its Social, Moral, and Economical Aspect," Mackay explored an American problem rapidly reaching a crisis, only a few years before the outbreak of the Civil War. After condemning the institution of slavery on every ground, social, moral, and economic,

Mackay concluded that "the peculiar condition of the Southern States is this, that they are afflicted with an evil which they fear to attempt the removal of; an evil already grown beyond their control, and increasing in magnitude every hour; an evil of which nothing but a social convulsion can rid them; which when it comes, as it assuredly will, may give rise to a political disposition of the continent as yet undreamed of." Mackay clearly foresaw a civil war as the only solution to slavery. He was mistaken, however, in predicting the likelihood of a split that would create two federal republics: "one in the North and the other in the South—the one free, the other slave holding."

Mackay was fully aware of the growth of American industry and of the nation's tremendous natural resources, mentioning specifically its forests, "fertile valleys and vast plains," mines rich in a variety of minerals, enormous territory, systems of lakes and rivers, extensive seacoast, numerous harbors, and geographical position—advantages that the British could not hope to match.

As a kind of postscript to the third and last volume of *The Western World,* Mackay added a chapter on California. After considering that state's strategic geographical position, its agricultural possibilities, and the recent discovery of gold, the author predicted that within twenty years the Atlantic and Pacific would be connected by railway, that there would be a rapid expansion of population along the West Coast, and that trade with Asia would expand. The United States would then become the stepping stone between Western Europe and Eastern Asia. "This will complete the political and commercial triumph of America."

In 1851, the chambers of commerce of the large northern cities of England sent Mackay to India to inquire into the possibility of raising cotton extensively in India. He died on the return voyage.

17. *Travels in North America; with Geological Observations on the United States, Canada, and Nova Scotia*

Sir Charles Lyell, widely regarded as the founder of the modern science of geology, made four trips to the United States. The first, lasting about one year, in 1841–42, was devoted almost entirely to geological research and led to his two-volume work, *Travels in North America.* Lyell returned a few years later, from September 1845 to May 1846, and again produced a detailed record of his travels, *A Second Visit to the United States of North America,* published in 1849. If any account of his last two visits—both shorter—in 1852 and 1853 was written, it has been lost.

While other sciences were moving ahead in the eighteenth and early nineteenth centuries, the progress of geology was seriously retarded. During this period, the biblical story of the Creation and the Flood remained the fundamental textbook of geology. Fossils were believed to be the remains of animals lost in Noah's Flood. Geologists in general held the view that the whole history of the earth consisted of a series of sudden and violent catastrophes by which the bed of the ocean was suddenly raised and its waters precipitated onto the land, carrying with them universal ruin and the extermination of all life. After each catastrophe, there would be periods of quiet, during which the new earth was repopulated, by direct act of creation, with new forms of life adapted to the new conditions. Species of life were unchanged until another cataclysm exterminated them. Still raging in Lyell's youth was the controversy between the Neptunists, who argued that the earth's crust was formed by layers deposited or precipitated by an ocean that once covered the entire surface of the globe, and the Vulcanists, who maintained that the earth's present contours are accounted for by volcanic action.

Into this debate came Lyell, with extraordinary talent for synthesizing the findings of other scientists and for interpreting all kinds of natural phenomena. The dominant idea in Lyell's writings is that geological causes can be discovered only by studying the forces at work on the earth today. His observed that mountains and continents are being built, strata are being folded and broken, igneous and sedimentary rocks are being formed, and fossils are being buried in the same manner now as in past ages. There have been no vast cataclysms or devastating floods. Thus arose the uniformitarian doctrine to oppose and eventually to discredit the apostles of catastrophism. Lyell's three-volume work, *Principles of Geology, Being an Attempt to Explain the Former Changes of the Earth's Surface, by Reference to Causes Now in Operation,* published in 1830–33, quickly became a classic. It served to blaze the trail for the later acceptance of Darwin's theory of evolution.

One of Lyell's contributions was to develop the nomenclature for geological eras—Eocene, Miocene, Pliocene, etc.—that has since been accepted worldwide.

Lyell was strongly convinced of the virtues of travel in advancing the progress of geology. As he declared, "travel is the first, second and third requisite for a modern geologist in the present adolescent state of the science." Before his first American tour and later, he traveled extensively in Europe. His journeys to America were intended to be primarily scientific in aim and were extremely productive. During the 1841–42 stay, about ten months were spent in active geological field work and two months in cities lecturing to large audiences. From that expedition, Lyell brought back a quantity of specimens and a mass of notes on the raised beaches of the Canadian lakes, the glacial drift, Niagara Falls, and other questions of post-tertiary geology, as well as on tertiary, cretacious, and older rocks.

It was said that a visit to America opened up a new world to Lyell. He was impressed to find that almost everything was on a colossal scale—rivers, lakes, forests, prairies, distances—unmatched in the parts of Europe with which he was familiar. America offered a tempting field for him. Large areas awaited exploration, and in many places the traveler found virgin territory. Geological surveys were in their infancy.

In 1832, Lyell married Mary Horner, a devoted and talented wife. Because of his seriously defective eyesight, she wrote many of his letters and other writings. She also accompanied him on practically all of his travels, including the American tours.

The Lyells landed in Halifax in July 1841, and from there proceeded to Boston and New Haven. In this district they found the grasshoppers as numerous and noisy as in Italy, watched the fireflies in the darkness, and caught their first sight of humming-birds. Their itinerary next took them to New York, up the Hudson past the Palisades, and then to Niagara. A thorough study was made of the Falls, during which Lyell estimated that they were receding at a rate of about a foot a year.

Continuing his travels, Lyell went on to Buffalo and Geneva; examined rock formations in New Jersey and bituminous and anthracite coal deposits in Pennsylvania and the Allegheny Mountains; and then returned to Philadelphia, New York, and Boston, where he delivered a series of lectures at Lowell Institute attended by as many as 3,000 persons. Thereafter Lyell took a southern route, stopping first at Richmond and the James River, where he inspected Miocene-age deposits. He was impressed with various features of the Great Dismal Swamp in North Carolina. Three weeks were spent in the Charleston area before the Lyells went back to Philadelphia and New York. A western trek took them across the Allegheny Mountains to Cincinnati, the famous Big Bone Lick in Kentucky, Cleveland, Lake Erie, and then into Canada. All along the route, Lyell gathered geological data. They returned to England in August 1842, after an absence of about twelve months.

Although Lyell's American missions were primarily scientific, he was a keen observer of social and political life in the United States. At the very outset of his book he remarked on the rapid growth of such cities as Utica, Syracuse, Auburn, and Rochester; the absence of want and poverty; the number of schoolhouses and churches; and the general desire for education. He was impressed by the extreme politeness shown toward women, who could travel anywhere without risk of encountering disagreeable behavior or hearing coarse language. He highly commended the general concept of religious freedom, with all religious sects having political and social equality.

Lyell's first observations on slavery were recorded during his visit to Charleston. Slave labor, he noted, was not really free, because slaves had to be fed, clothed, given medical attention, and closely supervised. Slaves had to carry passports, without which they were not permitted to be out after nightfall. As seen by Lyell, the slaves seemed "cheerful and free from care, better fed than a large part of the laboring class of Europe." In South Carolina, the blacks were a majority of the population and were increasing more rapidly than the whites.

Lyell found that the institution of slavery was most injurious to the progress of the whites, and "there appears to be no place in society for poor whites." He found depressing the contrast with the rapid advance of the same class of people in the North.

In reaction against the abolitionist movement and in fear of slave insurrections, Lyell noted strict laws against importing books relating to emancipation, against teaching slaves to read and write, and forbidding the return of slaves who had lived in free territory.

Lyell was well aware of the defects of universal suffrage, but he pointed to the New England states as evidence that general suffrage was compatible with order, obedience to law, security of property, and a high degree of civilization. He commented favorably on the existence of popular libraries in almost every village in Massachusetts, a growing taste for reading good books, and the sale of large editions of some works. Books were far cheaper and more available than in England, in part because of the lack of copyright protection for British authors.

In September 1845, the Lyells set out for another American tour. From Halifax, they went on to Boston and traveled in Maine and to the White Mountains, where they climbed Mount

Washington on horseback. Considerable space in the *Second Visit to the United States* is devoted to political, commercial, educational, and theological questions as well as to geological research. There are chapters on the witch-hunting mania in Massachusetts in the seventeenth century and folklore about sea serpents in the St. Lawrence River. An ambitious itinerary took the Lyells from Boston to New Haven, New York, Philadelphia, Washington, Richmond, Wilmington, Charleston, Savannah, Milledgeville, Macon, Montgomery, Mobile, and New Orleans. Side trips were made to Lake Pontchartrain and to the mouth of the Mississippi. Lyell gained some insights into the history of river deltas as he traveled northward some hundreds of miles along the Mississippi. Stops along the way back included Natchez, Vicksburg, Memphis, Louisville, and then across the Alleghenies to Philadelphia, New York, and Boston. In June 1846, the Lyells landed in Liverpool.

The *Second Visit,* in addition to descriptions of scenery and the geology of the country, contains much general information about the American people, the effects of universal suffrage, the evils of slavery, the state of religion, and the systems of education—all told through the eyes of a highly intelligent, articulate, unbiased, and sympathetic commentator.

18. *Travels in the United States in 1847*

The most notable and most admired Latin American to visit the United States in the nineteenth century was Domingo Faustino Sarmiento, an Argentine educator, author, journalist, and president of the Argentine republic. Because of his strong political opinions and opposition to the dictatorial regime of President Juan Manuel Rosas, he was imprisoned for propaganda. After escaping to Chile, he edited two newspapers, founded the first Chilean normal school, served on the faculty of the University of Chile, and became celebrated for his outspoken support of liberal government and public education.

Sarmiento's intense concern with public education inspired him to spend several years in Europe, Africa, and the United States to study educational methods. After helping to overthrow Rosas, he again returned to journalism and began an active campaign for public education. In 1862 he was elected governor of San Juan. Two years later, in 1864, Sarmiento served successively as minister to Chile and Peru, and in 1865 to the United States. While still in the United States, he was elected president of Argentina for the 1868–74 term. In that position, he broadened and completely reorganized the national system of public education. Toward the end of his long career, Sarmiento was made national superintendent of schools and was able to complete the principal features of his campaign for universal education.

Sarmiento was a prolific author. His complete works fill 52

volumes, several relating to the United States. An account of his first visit, *Travels in the United States in 1847,* was not translated until 1969. During a stay of less than two months starting September 15, 1847, Sarmiento traveled about the eastern part of the country, visiting all the major cities, and journeyed by stagecoach and by steamboat from Pittsburgh to New Orleans on the Ohio and Mississippi Rivers. He set sail for South America on November 4.

Running short of funds in the course of his earlier European travels, Sarmiento doubted that he could afford to go on to the United States, but he convinced himself, asking, "Could I as a schoolteacher on a world trip of exploration to examine the state of primary education return to South America without having inspected the schools of Massachusetts, the most advanced in the world? As a republican, and having witnessed what form the republic has taken in France, could I return without having seen the only great and powerful republic that exists on the earth today?" He resolved to get to the United States one way or another and to finance the rest of the trip by working his way, if necessary.

The highlight of Sarmiento's American visit undoubtedly was meeting and spending a considerable amount of time with the famous educator Horace Mann and his wife Mary. "The principal object of my trip," he wrote, "was to meet Mr. Horace Mann, Secretary of the Board of Education, the great reformer of primary education, who like myself had traveled through Europe in search of methods and systems, a man who combined an inexhaustible quantity of good will and philanthropy with a rare prudence and a profound wisdom in his acts and in his writings."

In a two-day visit, Mann and Sarmiento spent long hours discussing educational matters. Sarmiento spoke no English and Mann no Spanish. Mary Mann served as interpreter. Mann told of "his tribulations, and of the difficulties which beset his great work, such as popular prejudices on education, local and sectarian jealousies, and political interference." It is of interest to note that for some years after Horace Mann's death, Mrs. Mann and Sarmiento remained in close touch through correspondence and occasional visits. On his return to South America, Sarmiento carried copies of Mann's lectures, reports, and speeches. In 1865, he wrote that "during these years I have done nothing else but follow in his footsteps, his great work in organizing education in Massachusetts serving as my model."

Under Mary Mann's guidance, Sarmiento met the leading New England literary lights including Ralph Waldo Emerson, whom he greatly admired, and Longfellow, whose facility with the Spanish language was an asset.

Sarmiento began his *Travels in the United States* with what he called "A General Description" based on his having "visited all of her great cities and crossed or followed the borders of twenty-one of her richest states." In his view, the country possessed three prime requisites for becoming a great republic: unlimited territory for a future population of two hundred million inhabitants, a wide frontage on the seas, and a surface suitable for the development of railroads and canals. Also important, he thought, were navigable rivers and an abundance of building stones.

Sarmiento was amazed at the rapid rise of industrial cities in the United States: Pittsburgh (which he called "the Yankee Birmingham" because of it was "wrapped in a dense mantle of thick foul-smelling smoke"), Buffalo and other centers around the Great Lakes. Credit for these phenomenal growths was given to unlimited coal deposits in the region and to the ingenuity of Americans in utilizing natural resources, the proximity of major cities, and the construction of canals to link various areas in the Northeast and Middle West.

Another extraordinary feature of the United States, as seen by Sarmiento, was its villages, which he found to be the center of political life. "The American village," he stated, "is a small edition of the whole country, in its civil government, its press, its schools, its banks, its town hall, its census, its spirit, and its appearance"—unlike French and Chilean villages.

In the far western areas of the United States, Sarmiento noted, the level of civilization was more primitive because of the sparse population. Most homes were log houses that could be constructed very quickly. A striking feature of these frontier communities was the "appearance of perfect equality among the population in their dress, in their manners, and even in their intelligence."

Merchants, doctors, sheriffs, farmers all looked the same. Also noteworthy was the speed with which new ideas, devices, and inventions were adapted and spread to all parts of the country.

Nearly all Americans traveled, Sarmiento found, and transportation facilities were constantly improving and costs being reduced on macadam roads, railroad lines, or navigable rivers. Large steamboats on the Hudson River were cheap, elegantly furnished, served delicious meals, and even provided bridal suites.

"A country girl in the United States," remarked Sarmiento, "is distinguished from her city cousins only by her rosy cheeks, her round, plump face, and her frank and simple smile. Aside from this and a little less style and ease in the way she wears her shawl, she and all American women belong to the same class, and their good looks honor the human race."

Another aspect of American life that impressed Sarmiento was the grand hotels, which he described as "palaces." Every large city in the United States, he noted, "boasts of two or three monstrous hotels that compete among themselves in offering luxury and comfort to the public at the lowest prices." At meal functions in the hotels, there were three regulations to protect the women: "(1) No one may take a seat at the common table until the ladies, with their husbands or kinsmen, have occupied the head and adjacent sides of the table; (2) Guests are requested not to smoke or chew tobacco at the table; (3) At the sound of the bell, gentlemen may sit down in the remaining seats."

About one-third of Sarmiento's *Travels in the United States* is titled "Travel Incidents," a series of sketches of American cities that give the author's impressions of New York, Niagara, several Canadian communities, Boston, Baltimore, Philadelphia, Washington, Pittsburgh, Cincinnati, and New Orleans.

When Sarmiento was writing in 1847, fourteen years before the outbreak of the Civil War, he had serious premonitions about the outcome of the slavery controversy. "Everyone today is afraid that this colossus of a civilization," he wrote, "so complete and so vast, may die in the convulsions which will attend the emancipation of the Negro race." At the time of the Republic's founding, when the number of slaves was small, slavery could have been abolished, but "Washington and the great philosophers of the

Declaration of the Rights of Man made a fatal error when they allowed the Southern planters to keep their slaves." Sarmiento threw up his hands at this point and concluded "slavery in the United States is today a question without solution." On the basis of his travels, however, he was convinced that "the free states are superior in number and wealth to the slave states."

The last stop for Sarmiento's 1847 American tour was New Orleans, where he spent ten days before sailing for Havana on the first stage of his return to Argentina.

19. *The Homes of the New World; Impressions of America*

One of the most thorough of the foreign travelers who came to America in the mid-nineteenth century was a Swedish novelist, Frederika Bremer, the daughter of a wealthy ironmaster and merchant. Her literary career had began in 1828, when she published the first of several successful novels.

At the outset of her American tour, which began in the autumn of 1849, Bremer spent nearly a year along the Atlantic seaboard and in the South. Her first hosts in the United States were Andrew Jackson Downing, now recognized as the father of American landscaping, and his wife. From early October 1849 to March 1850, Bremer was received as a celebrity in New England and New York, and formed friendships with Ralph Waldo Emerson, Nathaniel Hawthorne, Henry Wadsworth Longfellow, Washington Irving, James Russell Lowell, William Cullen Bryant, James Greenleaf Whittier, Bronson Alcott, Margaret Fuller, and others. In her letters, Bremer also mentions the actress Fanny Kemble; scientist Asa Gray; such famous ministers as Ellery Channing, Henry Ward Beecher, and Theodore Parker; and the prominent abolitionists Wendell Phillips, Charles Sumner, and Frederick Douglass. She drew portraits of Emerson, Longfellow, and other celebrities to take back to Sweden.

Her fame gave Bremer universal welcome wherever she went. Her two-volume work is full of appreciation, but she also mentions frequently becoming exhausted by too much hospitality. She was "vexed to distraction" by insistent personal questions such as the following: "At the hotel at Buffalo I was again tormented by some new acquaintance with the old, tiresome questions, 'How do you like America?' 'How do you like the States?' 'Does Buffalo look according to your expectations?' To which latter question I replied that I had not expected anything from Buffalo."

The "pitiless hospitality" of Americans also drew complaints from Bremer. She wrote, "and that is the way they kill strangers in this country. They have no mercy on the poor lion, who must make a show and whisk his tail about as long as there is any life left in him. One must be downright obstinate and stern, if one would be at peace here. And I feel as if I should become so."

Bremer found food in America plentiful and of great variety, but noted that much of it was indigestible and injurious to weak stomachs.

The slavery controversy was raging in 1850, and Frederika Bremer made frequent references to it. She found the abolitionist movement in the North and the pro-slavery forces in the South equally unyielding and uncompromising. The more enlightened slaveholders recognized the evils of the institution, but could see no immediate solution. Bremer attended sessions of Congress and heard the heated debates led by Henry Clay and Daniel Webster to avert civil war by measures that constituted the Compromise of 1850.

During her stay in Washington in the summer of 1850, Bremer met the leading members of Congress, President Taylor, and other prominent government officials. She was unimpressed by congressional speeches, commenting, "in general, the speakers in this country scream too much; they are too violent, and shout and roar out their words as if they would be very powerful. Henry Clay is free from this fault, but he is evidently more impulsive and has less control over himself than Webster."

Bremer evidently had a deeply religious bent and refers often to witnessing religious services. She was curious about the nature and creeds of various denominations and sects; among the churches she visited and ceremonies she described were Unitarian, Quaker, Shaker, Catholic, and Baptist. She was impressed by camp meetings, in which thousands participated and hundreds were baptized by immersion. She also attended services in a number of black churches, where she was touched by the "enigmatical character, songs and religious festivals" of the members.

Bremer's southern travels began in Charleston and continued from March to June 1850. She was delighted with the "magnificent scenery" seen in the Carolinas and Georgia—the rivers, unspoiled forests, flowering creepers, and the "infinitely-picturesque beauty" of the land, "even though slavery and sandy deserts exist there." In Charleston, she was struck by "the great number of Negroes and the large flocks of turkey buzzards," the latter serving as city scavengers.

Summing up her observations on the northeastern states, Bremer "found there earnestness and labor, restless onward-striving, power both manual and spiritual, large educational establishments, manufactures, asylums for the suffering, and institutions for the restoration of fallen humanity . . . and, above all, the upward-progressive movement of society." She also admired the natural beauty of the rivers and the hills and valleys, which she compared to Sweden.

To round out her travels, Bremer next proceeded west to Chicago by way of Albany, Niagara, Rochester, Ontario, Buffalo, Detroit, Ann Arbor, and Lake Erie. "Chicago," she reported, "is one of the most miserable and ugly cities which I have yet seen in America, and is very little deserving of its name, 'Queen of the Lake' . . . she resembles rather a huckstress than a queen." This disparaging comment was made, of course, some years before Chicago burned and was rebuilt.

By the first of October, a year after leaving Sweden, Bremer arrived in Wisconsin and Minnesota. On the way, she saw the prairies for the first time and was rapturous in describing the great sea of grass with its birds, flowers, and undulating horizon. To her, the prairie was a sight less common and more magnificent than Niagara Falls. She was also delighted with the voyage up the Mississippi in October, noting especially the purity of the water and the rocky, vine-covered hills along the banks.

Scandinavians had populated the Wisconsin-Minnesota area by the time of Frederika Bremer's visit, and she was happy to hear her native language spoken by many inhabitants. In St. Paul, she was met by Governor and Mrs. Alexander Ramsey, in whose home she was a guest during her week's stay.

The local Indians were of particular interest to Bremer, and she took advantage of the opportunity to observe their physique, bearing, dress, dwellings, manner of life, sports and ceremonies, and the condition of the Indian women. A number of Indians were persuaded to pose for her sketches. Among those who posed for her were an old chief and a young woman attired in her wedding finery. The streets of St. Paul swarmed with Indians, fantastically painted and ornamented. As an ardent feminist herself, Bremer deplored the subjected state of the women, who in her eyes led a life of degradation as beasts of burden. On visits to several tepees, she discovered not dirt and poverty as anticipated, but a rude oriental splendor, colorful blankets and cushions, pipes, and hunting implements.

Near the end of her stay in Minnesota, Bremer attended a medicine dance in which about a hundred Indians participated, accompanied by the music of drums and gourds and the violent shaking of silver bells. The experience led her to reflect on Indians' religious life and to wonder about their theology.

Minnesota made a deep impression on Bremer, and she predicted the rise of a new Scandinavia there. As the American literary historian John T. Flanagan points out, "The facts that Minnesota contains the largest number of Swedes of any state in the Union and that Minneapolis is the largest Swedish city outside of Sweden prove the sanity and clairvoyance of Miss Bremer's view."

Bremer made her return trip by way of St. Louis and Cincinnati, where she reported on the operation of the underground railway for escaping slaves, and New Orleans, where she was deeply shocked to witness a slave auction of a mother and child. From New Orleans, she proceeded to spend from early February to April in Havana and several smaller Cuban communities, and continued on to Charleston, Savannah, Lake Monroe (Florida), Richmond, Charlottesville, Philadelphia, Boston and other New England communities, Saratoga, and New York City, about all of which she commented at length. She left New York bound for Liverpool on September 13, 1851, after nearly a two-year absence from Sweden.

Frederika Bremer's *The Homes of the New World; Impressions of America* was translated and published in London and New York almost as soon as it appeared in Sweden and attracted a large audience of readers in the United States.

Several years after her return to Sweden, Bremer undertook further travels. Beginning in 1856, she spent five years on the continent and in Palestine. In her later novels, she expounded her views on the emancipation of women.

20. *Travels in the United States, etc. during 1849 and 1850*

One of the most indefatigable travelers of the nineteenth century was Lady Emmeline Stuart-Wortley, daughter of the fifth Duke of Rutland. Her granddaughter wrote years later that Stuart-Wortley had a "constant longing to visit all parts of the world," and went far toward succeeding. She was also an exceptionally prolific writer, both of verse and prose, and wrote detailed accounts of her travels.

Before the death of her husband, Charles, in 1844, Lady Emmeline Stuart-Wortley visited many parts of Europe including Russia, where she made friends with Czar Nicholas II; Rome, where she met Napoleon's mother, Madame Letitia; Eastern Europe; and the Near East. By the time of her death in 1855, she had traveled on four continents. Her constant companion was her daughter Victoria, who was twelve when she and her mother came to the United States.

Stuart-Wortley and her daughter landed in New York in May 1849 and stopped at the Astor House, the mammoth size of which overwhelmed them. During the next stage of their trip, they proceeded to Albany on a Hudson River steamer described as a "perfect palace: a floating island of painting, marble, gilding, stained glass, velvet hangings, satin draperies, mirrors in richly-carved frames and sculptured ornaments, with beautiful vases of flowers and Chinese lamps." The fare was "marvellously small," less than one-sixth of a penny per mile. The Hudson was jammed with every variety of traffic.

117

Niagara Falls was, of course, a must and a more spectacular sight than usual because of two tremendous storms—"a vast black roaring cloud hanging over the white roaring wall."

The travelers spent the end of June back in New York, where, being British, they experienced mixed emotions when they saw a Fourth of July celebration. More disturbing, the city was in the grip of a record heat wave, and a cholera epidemic was increasing in severity. It seemed wise to move on to Boston. However the climate there was no improvement, and the travelers escaped to Gloucester, a "delectable place," where they enjoyed a fortnight in a new hotel, the Cape Ann Pavilion. Stuart-Wortley was intrigued by the dress of the American ladies; broad straw bathing hats, large white shawls, and elaborate fans were very popular. A passion for iced drinks, which she thought unhealthy, was universal.

Some features of Boston that most impressed the travelers were the clothing shops where merchandise was allowed to spill out on the sidewalks, the great wooden wharves and docks and tall ships, the long bridges, and the abnormal number of fires and fire-engines. On a visit to Cambridge, they were guided by President Edward Everett of Harvard University; met the celebrated scientist, Louis Agassiz; were guests in Daniel Webster's home; and met William Prescott, the historian of Mexico and Peru.

Before leaving for the South, Stuart-Wortley and her daughter spent a final week in New Haven. They were shown the treasures of Yale College by Professor Benjamin Silbiman, although it appears that they were most impressed by the din created by a plague of katydids, tree frogs, and crickets and by the vast quantities of peaches and tomatos that people consumed. Tomatos were deemed poisonous and were abhorred by Stuart-Wortley.

Carefully avoiding the sharp words of such preceding women travelers as Harriet Martineau and Frances Trollope, Lady Emmeline was filled with admiration for America. She made such comments as "America will evermore seem a second country to me," "the more I see of American society, the more I like it," and "it is all petty malice and jealousy which makes people talk of Americans' exaggerated expressions and ideas."

Concerning the most controversial subject of her time, the dispute between North and South, Stuart-Wortley's written opinions were discreet, although like other foreign travelers she recognized the potential of the conflict for splitting the federal union. She had confidence, however, that the central government was strong enough to suppress any rebellion.

Compared to British railroads, the travelers found American trains exceedingly slow, but they had high praise for water transportation, both by canal and by the great river steamboats.

On their way to Alabama and the Gulf, the travelers stopped over in Washington, where they were cordially received by President Zachary Taylor, whom they pronounced charming. Stuart-Wortley noted the "quick, keen, eagle-like expression in his eye." Worn down by the sectional conflict, they sensed that Taylor was "sorely tired of public life and the harassing responsibilities of his high office, and desired with passion to return to the quiet home on the banks of the Mississippi."

The travelers found the large number of slaves in Washington depressing, and thought that slavery "seemed strikingly out of place in the District of Columbia." Farther south, they viewed the slavery system in operation in Mississippi and Louisiana. Stuart-Wortley's reactions to this "peculiar institution" were mixed, because she saw both its good and evil aspects.

From Washington, the travelers headed for St. Louis. They crossed the Alleghenies in an antiquated stagecoach, experiencing an extremely uncomfortable trip because of a worn-out roadway, deep snow, and a reckless driver. Two days later they reached Cincinnati, a city "so unkempt and uncomfortable" that they hastened on to Louisville. Apartments in their river steamer, *The Fashion,* were commodious but infested by "a vast and convivial army of cockroaches."

In Louisville, another variety of animal life appalled them. As in New York, Washington, and Cincinnati, pigs filled the streets and sidewalks. Here, too, the travelers were disgusted by the American habit of chewing tobacco and spitting incessantly on street pavements and even on church floors.

A side-trip out of Louisville was made to see the Mammoth Cave of Kentucky, where they spent two days exploring its wonders, all described in detail. The travelers left Louisville in a steamer crowded with "slaves, children, chattels, and cattle." The junction of the Ohio and Mississippi Rivers at Cairo was "a scene that in its majesty and strength impressed them," but they could see no future for the little town of Cairo, which they called "one gigantic fever-trap."

St. Louis was finally reached. The city had lately been devastated by fire and cholera. A third of the inhabitants had been carried off by the pestilence, but the city was now in the middle of a building boom, and German immigrants were pouring in.

On December 5, 1849, the travelers boarded the *Bostona,* a luxurious steamer, to continue their voyage south on the Mississippi. Although beautifully equipped, such steamers frequently experienced catastrophes caused by engine explosions, collisions, fires, constant fogs, treacherous currents, and daredevil captains racing each other. Nevertheless, despite many dangers and discomforts, the great river had infinite variety, the travelers found its vastness inspiring. Along the shores could be seen busy wharves and landing-stages, growing villages and towns, scattered huts of woodcutters, many plantations, planters' mansions, and long rows of slave dwellings; on the river itself were numerous passenger steamers, slow moving freight boats, flatboats, and rafts. Night scenes were especially spectacular, as hundreds of lights twinkled along the shore and from passing steamers.

The *Bostona* discharged its passengers in Memphis during a snowstorm. After two days' wait in a hotel there, they continued on to Natchez on the *Bulletin,* the principal cargo of which was cotton. The climate was gradually turning tropical, and heat was becoming oppressive. South of Natchez the voyagers passed through a continuous forest of cypresses broken by an occasional cotton plantation. At Cypress Grove, the home of President Taylor, the English ladies were hospitably received by his son. The slaves on the Taylor plantation were found to be "as well fed, comfortably clothed, and kindly cared for in every way as possible, and seemed thoroughly happy and contented." A passing steamer picked Stuart-Wortley and her daughter up when they were ready to leave Cypress Grove and carried them on to New Orleans and the Verandah Hotel.

New Orleans was described in rapturous terms. The travelers were entranced by the port "crowded with vessels of all sorts," huge bales of cotton on the quays, and the ancient French heart of the city with its balconies, orange trees, and pillared verandahs with fantastic ironwork. To them, "the French quarter of New Orleans was Old Orleans with an added touch of Spanish grace and Parisian fashion." A great system of levees protected the city from drowning by the Mississippi.

The tropical heat of New Orleans was debilitating for the travelers, and they didn't regret, therefore, leaving it and steaming down Lake Pontchartrain to Mobile. There they were royally entertained by Madame LeVert, a close friend of Henry Clay. A visit was made to the neighboring camp of Choctaw Indians, some of whom Victoria sketched.

In the meantime, the travelers waited for a long-overdue English steamer to take them to Vera Cruz. When it failed to arrive, they accepted passage on a special boat that had been provided for the newly appointed U.S. Minister to Mexico. In their continuing itinerary, Stuart-Wortley and her daughter visited Mexico, Havana, the Isthmus of Panama, Panama City, the Pacific Coast, Peru, and Jamaica before returning to England and planning further travels.

21. *Autobiography*

For centuries Japan was a closed society. Interaction with the Western world was sporadic and intermittent. The Japanese government finally ordered that no Japanese might go abroad, and no foreigner might enter Japan except for a limited number of Dutch traders operating under special conditions. This isolation remained substantially unchanged until ships from the United States Navy, under the command of Commodore Matthew Perry, arrived in 1853. In the long interim this edict against dealing with all foreigners except the Dutch was strictly enforced by the shogun's government.

The American government, unhappy with the treatment of its ships that touched Japanese ports, finally decided to send a formidable force of ten naval vessels and two thousand men to in effect compel the Japanese to conclude a commercial treaty. At first, the Japanese were inclined to fight, but they finally decided that effective resistance was impossible. After some weeks of negotiations, a treaty of peace and friendship was signed. Among its stipulations were: The ports of Shimoda in Izu and Hakodate should be opened to United States ships, and Americans would be allowed to frequent the ports within definite limits; U.S. consuls or agents might reside in Shimoda; and shipwrecked sailors should be relieved, and ships might obtain fuel and provisions in Japanese territory. Russia, Holland, and England soon secured similar treaties. Thus, after a long period of enforced seclusion from the rest of the world, Japan entered the society of nations. Western ideas poured in: schools were founded; books were published; and the study of astronomy, geography, medicine, literature, architecture, and painting flourished.

Among the interested spectators of these developments was a young Japanese, Fukuzawa Yukichi, who lived at Nakatsu on the coast of Kyushu and was eighteen at the time of Commodore Perry's visit. His father belonged to the samurai class.

Although the Dutch had been active in Japanese commercial affairs for two-and-a-half centuries, no one in young Fukuzawa's town could understand the Dutch language, "the strange letters written sideways." The news of the appearance of the American fleet in Tokyo had made a strong impression on even the most remote towns in Japan. The problem of national defense and the new art of warfare were of foremost interest to the samurai. The study of gunnery could only be undertaken under Dutch instructors, which meant that the Dutch language must be learned. Fukuzawa had no particular concern for armaments; he saw the study of Dutch, however, as a way to get ahead in the world and to escape from the provincial village of Nakatsu, with which he was thoroughly bored. He went to Nagasaki, therefore, to become proficient in Dutch. At the time, Nagasaki, with its Dutch compound, was the only port in Japan in touch with the outside world.

Fukuzawa made fairly rapid progress in the study of Dutch, however a disagreement with the family with whom he lived caused him to go on to Tokyo, a distance of several hundred miles, which he traveled primarily on foot for lack of money. He made an intermediate stop in Osaka, where he continued the study of Dutch. Fukuzawa's principal means of learning was a German-Dutch dictionary that had been translated into Japanese.

In 1859, the year after Fukuzawa Yukichi reached Tokyo, the so-called Treaty of the Five Nations was signed, and the port of Yokohama was formally opened for trade with foreign countries. To his dismay, when Fukuzawa attempted to talk with merchants showing their wares in Yokohama, they were unable to understand him, or vice versa. He could neither read the signboards over the shops nor the labels on the bottles for sale. The strange new language used here was English. Fukuzawa was bitterly disappointed to discover that Dutch, which he had been studying so assiduously for years, was a minor language rather than the lingua franca that would admit him to an understanding of Western civilization.

The day after returning from Yokohama, Fukuzawa resolved to begin the study of English. However, not a single English teacher was to be found in Tokyo. By good fortune, a Dutch-English dictionary and a small English conversation book were procured, and Fukuzawa started forming English sentences from the Dutch dictionary. He drew upon the knowledge of anyone who might know English pronunciations, such as shipwrecked Japanese fishermen who were brought back on foreign vessels. He found that his study of Dutch had not been in vain; there were enough similarities between Dutch and English to facilitate learning the latter.

The year after Fukuzawa settled in Tokyo, 1859, he received an opportunity for foreign travel. "The government of the Shogun," he wrote in his *Autobiography,* "made a great decision to send a ship-of-war to the United States, an enterprise never before attempted since the foundation of the empire. On this ship I was to have the good fortune of visiting America." The so-called warship was actually a small sailing craft equipped with an auxiliary steam engine of one hundred horsepower, to be used for maneuvering in and out of harbors. In the open sea, the ship had to depend entirely on sail. The Japanese government had purchased her from the Dutch a few years before and named her the *Kanrin-Maru.*

Japanese officers and crews had been preparing for the voyage by studying navigation and the operation of steamships since the opening of ports in 1855. Help had been secured from Dutch residents at Nagasaki, and now the Japanese felt themselves qualified to take a ship across the Pacific to San Francisco as an escort for the American warship carrying Japan's first envoy to Washington. The entire crew totaled ninety-six men, larger than usual for the ship. It was an epoch-making adventure for the Japanese nation. Every member of the crew was determined to make the voyage unassisted by any foreigner in order to gain full honors for its anticipated success.

Through influential connections, Fukuzawa Yukichi was granted "his greatest wish," to be taken along on the voyage, and served as personal steward to the captain. In January 1860, the *Kanrin-Maru* left Tokyo (Yedo) from the shores of Shinagawa, one of the city's ports on Tokyo Bay.

After leaving Tokyo Bay, the small ship sailed on a far northern route. No sooner did it get into the open sea than it ran into storms; rough weather continued all the way across. It was practically impossible to eat sitting down at a table; Fukuzawa piled his rice in a bowl, poured soup and all other food over it, and ate standing up.

The bowl, a large china one, Fukuzawa had "purloined" from a restaurant where the envoy had held a party to celebrate their leave-taking. "That bowl proved to be about the most convenient article I brought along on the voyage." He used it daily until the ship reached America, and again on the return trip. "Finally I took the bowl home and it remained in my homestead for a long time . . . later . . . I heard that the place where we had celebrated . . . was a place of rendezvous for prostitutes with their customers. I did not suspect it at the time, but very probably my bowl had served as a toilet accessory for the gay ladies of the house. That made me squirm a bit when I learned it. . . . "

On a tempestuous winter sea, the *Kanrin-Maru* faced the voyage under sail, without aid from the steam engine. Two of four lifeboats were lost overboard; storms followed each other and waves continually broke over the decks. At times the ship was tilted by as much as thirty-eight degrees. A sharper list would probably have capsized her and sent her to the bottom, but she kept her course. For a month the crew saw nothing but waves and clouds except for a single American vessel carrying Chinese workmen to the United States.

Near the end of the voyage, the ship's supply of water began to run low, and the question of making port in the Hawaiian Islands was considered. It was finally decided to go straight on to San Francisco, and by restricting the crew's water the voyage was completed without a stop. The ship reached San Francisco after thirty-seven days at sea. Fukuzawa expressed pride in the achievement of his fellow countrymen. The Japanese had never seen a steamship until 1853; two years later they began to learn about navigation from the Dutch at Nagasaki; and five years after that they were proficient enough to sail a ship across the Pacific.

When the *Kanrin-Maru* docked at San Francisco, many important persons came aboard to greet the company, and thousands of people lined up along the shore to see the strange newcomers. The ship's navigator returned a salute fired on shore. Americans seemed to feel a personal pride in the Japanese visit, for it was their Commodore Perry who had opened Japan to the world eight years earlier. All kinds of hospitality was extended to the visitors including special entertainment, an official residence at the naval station on Mare Island, food prepared Japanese fashion, and placing the ship in dry dock for repairs before it began its return voyage.

The customs and habits of American life were of course unknown to the Japanese, and some confusion and embarrassing moments ensued. For example, the visitors had never ridden in horse-drawn vehicles. The Japanese were amazed to see Americans walking on hotel floors covered with valuable carpets and rugs without removing their shoes. Another shock awaited them when champagne was served with ice cubes floating in the glasses. Some of the Japanese swallowed the frozen particles, others "expelled them suddenly," and others chewed them up. On another occasion, the visitors were invited to a dancing party and found it amusing to see "the ladies and gentlemen hopping around the room together." The greatest surprise of all came when they were invited to have dinner at the home of a prominent local physician and the main course was a whole pig, roasted head, legs, tail, and all.

Fukuzawa was inclined to be critical of the Americans for their wastefulness. He noted an enormous waste of iron everywhere, such as old oil tins, empty cans, and broken tools—items that would have been treasured in metal-poor Japan. Perhaps related to such waste was the high cost of standard commodities in California, far above prices in Japan. Things social, political, and economic proved inexplicable to Fukuzawa, and "One day, on a sudden thought, I asked a gentleman where the descendants of George Washington might be. He replied, 'I think there is a woman who is directly descended from Washington. I don't

know where she is now, but I think I have heard she is married.'"
Because he was accustomed to the reverence in Japan for ancestors and for founders of lines of great rulers, Fukuzawa found this
casual answer appalling.

A naval salute marked the departure of the *Kanrin-Maru* for
home. Fukuzawa's last purchase before leaving was a Webster's
dictionary, the first, he believed, to be imported into Japan. En
route the ship stopped several days in Hawaii to take on a supply
of coal. Fukuzawa was little impressed by the Hawaiian natives.
To him, they appeared to be barbarians, and their general state
"pretty miserable," while the king and queen showed no signs of
royalty.

Two years after Fukuzawa's return from his initial visit to
America, he was offered a second chance for foreign travel. The
Japanese government sent him as an official interpreter with a
group of Japanese envoys aboard an English vessel, the *Odin.*
The ship's itinerary included ports of call in Europe, Asia, and
Africa, with its return journey retracing their course through the
Mediterranean and the Indian Ocean. The mission reached Japan
after nearly a year of traveling.

Fukuzawa's third and last voyage to foreign lands was made in
1867, again to the United States. The purpose of the mission was
to complete the purchase of the second of two warships for
which the Japanese government had previously contracted. By
this time, a regular packet service had been opened between
Japan and America, and the Japanese delegation traveled on the
Colorado, of which Fukuzawa wrote: "It was a fast steamer of four
thousand tons, veritably palatial in comparison with the small
boat on which I had previously crossed." On this trip only
twenty-two instead of thirty-seven days were required to reach
San Francisco. Another ship was taken to Panama, where the
isthmus was crossed by train, and a third ship provided transportation to New York, from which the Japanese proceeded at once
to Washington. They completed the deal for the warship plus
several thousand rifles and sailed home the following year, in
1868.

Back in Japan, Fukuzawa found the sentiment against foreigners growing in bitterness and intensity. There was wide-

spread fear of exploitation by the Western world, and students and interpreters of the West and Western languages were subjected to threats and bullying. A lack of skill in diplomatic procedures, together with the language barriers, caused the Japanese to do violence to English subjects. There was also a return of the warlike spirit and the worship of ancient warriors. Inside the country there was much civil strife between conservatives and liberals who wanted to introduce new thoughts, new ideals into the Japanese culture. Eventually, political assassinations of high officials with pro-Western inclinations were increasingly common. Fukuzawa's outspoken speeches and writings favoring close connections with the West caused him to be subjected to a certain amount of discipline by the government and to run the risk of being killed by extremists. As evidence of the prejudice against aliens, he cited the case of the Duke of Edinburgh, who arrived at the palace in Tokyo to pay a formal visit. After much discussion concerning the propriety of conducting a foreign visitor into the imperial presence, it was deemed necessary to conduct an elaborate purification ceremony before the English aristocrat crossed the bridge over the moat to the castle.

Fukuzawa's later career was distinguished. His Tokyo school eventually became Keio University, one of Japan's most notable centers of higher education and probably the most Western-oriented of Japanese universities. Feeling the lack of a proper medium for transmitting his ideas and ideals to the general public, in 1882 Fukuzawa also established an influential newspaper, the *Jifi-Shimpo*. The breadth of view derived from his foreign travels were reflected in both enterprises.

22. *American Notes*

Charles Dickens was not quite thirty when he first visited America in 1842. He was already the author of a half dozen novels; extremely popular at home and abroad; and the creator of the beloved Pickwick, Oliver Twist, Barnaby Rudge, Nicholas Nickleby, and Little Nell.

As "The Literary Guest of the Nation," Dickens was received with tremendous enthusiasm in America. In Boston, his hotel was crowded with deputations from other cities and states begging for the honor of a visit. In New York, the ceremonial Dickens dinner, at which Washington Irving presided and Bryant spoke, was the greatest event of its kind since the Lafayette tour. Tickets for Dickens's public receptions sold at fabulous prices, and the press reported his every move.

Naturally, there was keen popular anticipation when it became known that Dickens was writing an account of his American experiences. Nineteen hours after a copy of *American Notes* reached New York in 1842, it had been reprinted and was on sale. Within two days the New York publishers had sold 50,000 copies. After being the recipient of so much lavish hospitality, it had been expected that Dickens would have only kind words for the young republic. His sharp criticisms on some aspects of American society therefore aroused resentment and anger and were widely regarded as a breach of good manners.

A brief outline of Dickens's itinerary during his several months in the United States reveals the scope of his travels. Visits in Boston, Lowell, Worcester, New York, and Philadelphia were followed by Washington (where he attended a session of Congress and was a guest of President Tyler at the White House). He went no farther south than Richmond and Baltimore, after which he traveled through York, Pittsburgh, Cincinnati, Columbus, and Cleveland to Buffalo, Niagara, and Montreal.

In *American Notes,* Dickens chiefly emphasized three criticisms: on copyright, the penal system, and slavery. The United States had refused to make a reciprocal agreement with Great Britain over international copyright. Therefore, any American publisher was free to steal the fruit of an English author's brain by publishing his or her books without payment. Not until 1892, long after Dickens's time, did the United States sign an international copyright convention. Nevertheless, his outspoken comments on the situation stirred bitter comments in the American press.

Concerning the penal system, the Philadelphia scheme of solitary confinement was believed to be a model, but Dickens denounced it as inhuman and asserted that the men administering the system did not fully realize what they were doing—thereby arousing the ire of many Philadelphians.

On the question of slavery, Dickens ridiculed the notion that public opinion would prevent any real cruelty to the slaves. There was overwhelming evidence, he was convinced, that slaves were at the mercy of cruel masters who were quite unrestrained by public sentiment.

To balance his criticisms, Dickens offered many compliments to his American hosts, acknowledging the hospitality of many citizens; complimented Boston's brightness, cleanness, and general attractiveness; declared that "the public institutions and charities of this capital city of Massachusetts are as nearly perfect as the most considerate wisdom, benevolence, and humanity can make them"; praised Dr. S. G. Howe's work with the dumb and blind; and compared favorably the factories at Lowell with the mills of Manchester.

Comments on New York were more critical. Dickens was appalled by the Tombs prison, where the inmates were kept without exercise or light, and by the swine that wandered the streets. At the same time he had kind words for the community's energy, the gay dress of the people, and the public squares.

Philadelphia was rated "a handsome city," and Dickens enjoyed its society.

American Notes is descriptive rather than analytical. Generalizing, however, Dickens concluded that Americans had a dull and gloomy character, were too suspicious and jealous of one another, were too addicted to "smart" business dealings, and were overly devoted to trade, leaving them too little time to devote to cultural and social refinements. To offset these weaknesses, Dickens also found Americans "by nature, frank, brave, cordial, hospitable, and affectionate." Never in his travels, he reported, did he see a woman "exposed to the slightest act of rudeness, incivility, or even inattention."

Dickens reserved his most critical judgments for the West. On a Pennsylvania canal boat he encountered "a perfect storm and tempest of spitting"; a fellow traveler was inordinately curious about his clothing; northern Ohio inns were infested with bugs; and he found the prairies monotonous, the Mississippi River a muddy stream with low, unhealthy looking banks, and St. Louis "an unhealthy swamp." On the other hand, Pittsburgh was "beautifully situated," Cincinnati was "a beautiful city, cheerful, thriving and animated," and Columbus was "clean and pretty."

More offensive to Americans than *American Notes* was Dickens's novel with an American theme, *Martin Chuzzlewit,* published two years after the author's return to England. It satirizes land speculation and gives an unflattering picture of the American frontier. The excesses of the American yellow press are ridiculed from the opening pages. The ludicrous aspects of private and domestic life, manners, and customs are similarly portrayed: tobacco chewing and spitting, picking teeth in public, men wearing their hats indoors, bolting food, indifference to the arts and graces of life, too-hot houses, and streets full of pigs. The hero of *Martin Chuzzlewit* buys a tract of land in Illinois, "Eden," only to find on his arrival that the place is a "hideous swamp, choked with slime and matted growth."

Angry Americans condemned *Martin Chuzzlewit* in the strongest terms. Dickens's New York friend Philip Howe, who had defended *American Notes,* felt let down by *Chuzzlewit* and called it an "indefensible, ungrateful, and exceedingly foolish libel." Other critics, American and British, were just as uncomplimentary.

In his *America Through British Eyes,* however, the eminent American historian Allan Nevins maintains that "The resentment of Americans was the greater from their knowledge that Dickens was perfectly honest, and that he had the ear of the world and of posterity." Our prowess in tobacco spitting was as appalling as he represented it to be, many crooked politicians owed their positions to corrupt party machines, the sensational press was held in low esteem, duels and assassinations were frequent, and many saw Broadway's pigs as disgusting.

The difference was that Americans did not want their faults revealed to the world in such shocking detail by a famous foreign critic.

Two years after the end of the Civil War, in 1867, Dickens made a second visit to the United States, long after resentments against *American Notes* and *Martin Chuzzlewit* had died down. This time he confined himself to giving a series of public readings from his works. Dickens had been doubtful about his reception, but everywhere he was given a most cordial reception and returned home wealthier by 20,000 pounds from the crowds that came to see and to hear him. At a public dinner given him in New York he expressed regret for any apparent unkindnesses in his writings and his heartfelt friendship for the United States. But if Dickens had indeed changed his mind on the New World, he never published his revised opinions.

23. *With Thackeray in America*

William Makepeace Thackeray never wrote an account of his travels in America, although he spent six months on a lecture tour in the United States in 1852–53. Before leaving England, he had made a tentative agreement with his London publisher, George Smith, for a book on the United States, but his other commitments allowed him no time for the project. Instead, it was left to Eyre Crowe, the secretary who accompanied Thackeray on his travels, to write an entertaining story of their adventures overseas. This book, *With Thackeray in America,* was not published until 1893, forty years later. Of added interest are Crowe's graphic pen and ink sketches of many scenes.

Several years before crossing the Atlantic, Thackeray had determined to lecture in the United States. A prime objective was to rebuild the family fortune that he had lost as a young man. When in the summer of 1852 the Boston publisher James T. Fields invited him to cross the ocean, Thackeray agreed at once. Shortly thereafter, a second invitation came from William Felt of the New York Mercantile Library Association.

On October 30, 1852, Thackeray and Crowe left Liverpool and disembarked at Boston on November 12. There was some uncertainty about how they would be received. James Gordon Bennett's *New York Herald* carried an editorial headed "Another Cockney Character Coming Over," and was critical of the sponsors for making the United States ridiculous by inviting such a "literary snob" as Thackeray to visit the country. Nevertheless, Fields and his friends arranged a cordial welcome at the Tremont House for their distinguished guest.

Thackeray's first series of lectures was scheduled in New York four days later. He passed the interim meeting Boston notables and attending a concert given in his honor. On the train to New York, Thackeray had the experience of meeting a newsboy selling cheap reprints of early Thackeray works in Appleton's Popular Library.

Despite misgivings on Thackeray's part, his lectures were well received. The first one, on November 19, drew an audience of 1,500, including most of the city's literary and professional celebrities, among George Bancroft, William Cullen Bryant, Horace Greeley, Washington Irving, and leaders of society. There was some criticism in the religious press, however, over Thackeray's choice of authors to discuss before mixed audiences, among them "some of the most objectionable writers in all English literature."

On the whole, Thackeray's lectures were highly successful. A second series was scheduled in New York in December and four lectures in Brooklyn. Thackeray was amazed at the public interest in him as a personality; critics frequently commented on his appearance and manner. Bryant, for example, wrote, "few expected to see so large a man; he is gigantic, six feet four at least; few expected to see so old a person; his hair appears to have kept its silvery record over fifty years . . . the expression of his face grave and earnest; his address perfectly unaffected and such as we might expected to meet within a well bred man somewhat advanced in years." Thackeray was also amused to read in the New York papers extraordinary accounts of his life and character.

Thackeray's triumphal tour was unaffected by such trivial matters. He was invited everywhere. He went to dinner before his lectures, to parties afterward, and received visitors and wrote notes all day. He met most of the leading men of New York and made profitable contacts with publishers. He particularly enjoyed social activities in such organizations as the Century Association.

After New York, Thackeray spent several weeks back in Boston to present six lectures and went on to Providence for three. The newspapers were less favorable in that area than in New York, but the lectures attracted large audiences and were judged a success from the start. His circle of acquaintances continued to expand and included the historian William H. Prescott; the historian of Spanish literature, George Tichnor; Richard Henry Dana; Oliver Wendell Holmes; Henry Wadsworth Longfellow; and James Russell Lowell.

From Boston, Thackeray proceeded to Philadelphia, accompanied on the last lap of the trip by Washington Irving. Most of February was devoted to lectures in Baltimore and Washington. His expectations for an enjoyable stay in Washington were fully realized. The British Ambassador, Philip Crampton, proved most hospitable; Edward Everett, secretary of state, gave a party for him; Senator Hamilton Fish gave a dinner in his honor; and he dined with President Millard Fillmore at the White House. Fillmore and Franklin Pierce, who was to succeed to the presidency in March, attended Thackeray's lecture together.

At the end of February, Thackeray left Washington to continue his lecture tour and spent March in Richmond, Charleston, and Savannah, his first direct contact with the southern institution of slavery. Until that point, Thackeray had reserved comments on the slave system, wishing to avoid stirring up southern resentment and thereby endangering the success of his lectures. *Uncle Tom's Cabin* had been published a year earlier, and feelings in the North and the South continued to run high. Thackeray did not find the blacks personally or physically attractive, although he "denied any white man's right to hold this fellow-creature in bondage and make goods and chattels of him and his issue."

The Richmond lectures had been arranged by John Reuben Thompson, editor of the *Southern Literary Messenger,* and were enthusiastically received. Only one unpleasant incident marred the stay. Eyre Crowe had gone into a slave market and had started to sketch some of the blacks placed on the auction block. A gang of angry whites gathered and threatened her, and she was forced to quit. In Charleston, Thackeray and Crowe went to a "black ball" to watch the dancing. In Charleston, too, they enjoyed the company of the famous scientist Louis Agassiz, who was also on a lecture tour. The final stop of the tour was in Savannah, where Thackeray visited a nearby plantation and inspected slave housing. Under the rationing system, he noted, the blacks were allotted "half a pound of bacon a day, plenty of flour, nice treacle, and a little tobacco."

Before beginning his American tour, Thackeray had read the books of other English travelers—Dickens, Captain Marryat, Harriet Martineau, Mrs. Trollope, and others. He decided that "its all exaggeration about this country—barbarism, eccentricites, nigger cruelties, and all." He learned "to sympathize with a great hearty nation of 26 millions of English speakers."

Thackeray sailed from New York on April 20, 1853, and landed at Liverpool on May 2.

24. *A Russian Looks at America . . . The Journey in 1857*

British writers' work has always predominated among narratives by foreign travelers in America; French and German authors are also well represented. The first comprehensive study of the United States in the Russian language, however, was the work of Aleksandr Borisovich Lakier, a thirty-two-year-old jurist, bureaucrat, and historian who traveled all over the United States in 1857 gathering material for his book.

Lakier brought to his interpretation of the American scene a point of view vastly different from that of English, French, and German travelers. His background was the Russia of the Czars Nicholas I and Alexander II, a nation a century behind Western Europe in social and political affairs and characterized by a long tradition of ruthless censorship. Lakier was fluent in French, German, Spanish, and English and learned in law, history, and economics.

The America that Lakier viewed was still chiefly agricultural, but the industrial revolution was beginning. The countryside was rural, but a score of cities were growing at a spectacular rate. Although the nation was theoretically thoroughly committed to social equality, slavery was strongly entrenched over a large area in 1857, and its defenders were ready to fight for its preservation.

Lakier was immediately conscious of the striking contrasts between the United States and his native land. In Russia, autocracy and serfdom were the prevailing system. A great void separated an educated elite from an illiterate peasant majority; the undeveloped economy was marked by backwardness and inefficiency; the administration of government was monopolized by an entrenched, arrogant, and often corrupt bureaucracy; and there was no public education for children of all social levels. The majority of judges was nearly illiterate, and bribery among judicial personnel was common.

Against this background, Lakier came to admire the United States, and his praise of American institutions, with the exception of slavery, was evidently intended to suggest models worthy of emulation in Russia.

Lakier's *A Russian Looks at America,* a two-volume work, is extremely detailed and factual. He assumed that his Russian readers would be almost totally ignorant of the United States and its history, government, institutions, and people. More than a hundred pages, therefore, are devoted to the history of the American colonies and to the Constitution of the United States.

In his search for information Lakier became the first Russian private citizen to travel widely through most of the United States east of the Mississippi. For five months during the summer, fall, and early winter of 1857, he journeyed by coastal steamer, railroad, horse-drawn carriage, and river steamboat from the Northeast to the Old Northwest, from the Upper Mississippi to New Orleans, and from Florida up along the entire Southeast coast. He visited Boston, New York, Philadelphia, Pittsburgh, Cincinnati, Louisville, Chicago, St. Louis, Memphis, New Orleans, and Washington. Filled with curiosity and seemingly inexhaustible energy, he made friends with farmers, fur traders, soldiers, factory workers, and miners in the North and Midwest, and visited southern plantations. Everywhere he went, he took full notes and kept a careful diary.

A feature of American life that particularly intrigued Lakier was the system of constitutional government with its separation of powers, checks and balances, guarantees of civil liberty, personal freedom, and trial by jury. It was the basis, Lakier felt, for peace, order, and freedom for Americans. The Constitution assured national unity while allowing diversity among individual states.

Condemnation of Russia's greatest social evil, serfdom, was strongly implied by Lakier's abhorrence of American slavery, which he called a "hateful ulcer in a free society." This "peculiar institution" was damned not only on moral grounds, but also as the chief obstacle to the South's economic growth and development. He emphasized the wastefulness and inefficiency of slave labor compared to free labor; for example, he blamed on slavery the failure of St. Louis to match Cincinnati and Chicago in prosperity. Lakier compared the haphazard tilling of plantations in Maryland and Kentucky unfavorably to the careful cultivation of farms in the nonslave states of Pennsylvania and Ohio. In Lakier's words, "large estates tilled by unfree labor cannot prosper as quickly as small farms cultivated by their owners."

Much of Lakier's attention was devoted to the consideration of other American institutions. The American court system, especially the principle of trial by jury, won his praise. On the basis of trials witnessed in Boston, he emphasized the independence of the judiciary and the efficiency, openness, and fairness of trial by jury in contrast to the cumbersome, corrupt, and secretive procedure of the Russian judiciary.

Equally worthy of emulation in Lakier's opinion was the American system of public education. "Straight from school," he pointed out, "pupils bring into real life the principles of democratic freedom and the ideas of self-government which will guide them for the rest of their lives." He was also impressed by the fact that both girls and boys attended primary and secondary schools, unlike Russia where women were trained only in domestic affairs. Lakier commended American schools' emphasis on training for practical life.

In addition to courts and schools, Lakier was concerned with American prisons and visited them at every opportunity. The Pennsylvania and Auburn systems were of special interest to him. Typical modes of punishment in Russia were exile and corporal punishment, whereas in America he found that rehabilitation was the principle of the best penal systems.

Lakier liked the openness of public buildings and institutions such as schools, libraries, courts, prisons, welfare institutions, and even the Military Academy at West Point and the White House. There was little red tape, and Lakier was apparently never denied permission to visit any public institution that he wished.

Among American characteristics Lakier noted were constant "running after the golden idol," the opportunity for poor people to get ahead, the prevailing spirit of egalitarianism, a general desire for self-improvement, and a pervasive restlessness and optimism. He described the American transportation system with admiration. At the time he was writing in 1857, the United States had thirty thousand miles of railroad track, whereas Russia had less than eight hundred.

Lakier was fascinated by, and somewhat sentimental about, Indians. The Indians of the northern plains were dwindling in number and were doomed to disappear, in part because of their inability to adapt to new ways. As Naomi Bliven wrote in reviewing the Lakier work, "the decisive factor was time: the energy unleashed by American independence drove settlers across this continent so fast that there were never any borderlands in which several generations of white men and Indians could meet and accustom themselves to each other."

Comparisons between the observations of Lakier and Alexis de Tocqueville are a favorite theme of critics. A quarter of a century separated their visits, but there are striking similarities between their impressions of mid-nineteenth-century America. Tocqueville was twenty-six, Lakier thirty-two. Both were trained in law, were historians, and experienced civil servants. They agreed that the principle of equality was a fundamental feature of American society. They both studied American prisons with a view to finding a more humane penal and prison system for Europe. Other features of American life and institutions on which the two highly perceptive travelers saw eye to eye were the independence of juries and judges, the high standards of public and private morality, the respect given women, the high standards of public education, and the literacy of all classes of society.

At the same time, the two commentators had different points of view. Tocqueville met primarily with high officials such as presidents, senators, and judges and such intellectuals as university presidents, scholars, and men of letters. Lakier met and fraternized with a much wider cross-section of American society. Henry Steele Commager called Lakier "a superb reporter, Tocqueville a philosopher." Lakier saw more clearly than Tocqueville the significance of the western movement and of the frontier as a melting pot and school for democracy. Both viewed slavery as a future threat to the Union, but Lakier was even more revolted by the moral aspects of the institution than was the Frenchman.

Lakier concluded that although "one may not love certain particulars in America, one cannot help loving America as a whole or being amazed at what it has that Europe cannot measure up to." He predicted that Americans would influence Europe "by the strength of their inventions, their trade, and their industry. And this influence will be more durable than any conquest."

25. *The City of the Saints and Across the Rocky Mountains to California*

By the time Richard Burton visited America in 1860, when he was just short of forty, he had become an international celebrity. His versatility was astounding: soldier, explorer, ethnologist, archaeologist, poet, translator, linguist, and also an amateur physician, botanist, zoologist, and geologist of some distinction. As a result of various foreign assignments, he was fluent in such exotic languages as Hindustani, Marathi, Sindhi, Punjabi, Persian, and Arabic, and reasonably proficient in Turkish, Armenian, Telugu, and Pashto.

Burton's record as an explorer was equally spectacular. He penetrated the Moslem holy shrine of Mecca; visited another holy and forbidden city, Harar, the capital of Somaliland; found the source of the White Nile; and discovered two great African lakes, Tanganyika and Victoria. Always a prolific writer, Burton achieved enduring fame with his monumental translation of the *Arabian Nights,* a sixteen-volume work. Before middle age, the historian H. H. Bancroft observed, Burton had "compressed into his life more of study, more of hardship, and more of successful enterprise and adventure, than would have sufficed to fill up the existence of half a dozen ordinary men."

Exactly why Burton chose to visit America is unknown; perhaps he was restless and somewhat at loose ends. A likely objective, given his consuming interest in various religions, was a study of Mormonism. The London *Times,* in 1855, had described Mormonism as "the most singular phenomenon of modern times," a conglomeration of "Judaism, Mohammedism, socialism, despotism, and the grossest superstition." It naturally invited further study by Burton, who had previously seen the holy cities of Rome, Mecca, Jerusalem, and Benares.

Burton left for America in April 1860. There is little record of his movements after he arrived, but he is known to have been in Canada, to have visited Washington, D.C., and possibly to have traveled in some of the southern states. On August 7, he began a three-week stagecoach ride from St. Joseph, Missouri, to Salt Lake City. He carried with him a silk hat in a hatbox, an umbrella, an English tweed shooting jacket, a pocket-sextant, a telescope, some tea, sugar, cognac, cigars, opium, and two revolvers. His traveling companions were a federal judge, a state marshal, and an artillery officer accompanied by his wife and infant daughter. He seems to have thoroughly enjoyed the trip across the plains and to have used the opportunity to study American Indians.

One aspect of the American scene that particularly fascinated Burton, with his unusual linguistic background, was the idiom of the people and Western jargon. He paid special attention to local dialects and such expressions as "neck of the woods," "criks," and "having a high old time of it," and noted a lawyer who "hung out his shingle." He learned different slang words for whiskey such as tarantula juice, red-eye, strychnine, corn-juice, Jersey lightning, and leg stretches. He could inform his English friends that the "big drink" was the Mississippi River, corn was maize, and biscuits were crackers. Also, such expressions as "knocked up" (English for fatigued) should not be used in the presence of American women.

Burton enjoyed new sights such as covered wagons, "those ships of the great American Sahara which, gathering in fleets at certain seasons, conduct the traffic between the eastern and western shores of a waste which is everywhere like a sea and which presently will become salt. They are not unpicturesque from afar, these long winding trains, in early morning like lines of white cranes trooping slowly over the prairie." He also saw the Pony Express, which had been in operation for only five months.

Burton was put off by heavy American breakfasts, "the eternal eggs and bacon." The man who had endured the primitive fare of India, Arabia, and Central Africa complained of thick rashers of bacon and of vile coffee.

Burton talked with everyone he met and made copious notes about everything that he saw or heard. In the first third of his book, *The City of the Saints,* he included descriptions of the Indians he encountered, a graphic essay on the art of scalping, a comparison of African and Indian totemism, and a detailed account of Indian sign language. He noted that the "red man" was not red at all, but rather was like "a Tartar or an Afghan after a summer march," or the Mongolians he had seen in northern India. The Indian rode his horse, according to Burton, "like the Abyssinian eunich, as if born upon and bred to become part of the animal." The Sioux practice of cutting off the nose of an adulterous woman came as no surprise—he had seen the same practice in Hindustan. Burton viewed the Indians' religion as fetishism or totemism, and the medicine man as "sorcerer, prophet, physician, exorciser, priest and rain-doctor." He concluded that the common Indian beliefs in the Great Spirit and in an afterlife had recent antecedents—the result of missionary teaching. Close association with whites along emigrant trails was a corrupting influence, Burton noticed, often leading Indians to become beggars, liars, horse thieves, and prostitutes. Further, "poverty, disease, and debauchery rapidly thin the tribesmen."

Burton refused to romanticize the mountain men, calling them superstitious and transcendental liars.

After nineteen days of coach travel, Burton reached Salt Lake City. He responded emotionally as the coach emerged from the last canyon and the Mormon city could be seen in a great valley. He was truly awed and made comparisons with scenes from Switzerland and Italy. From a distance he thought the city had an oriental aspect and in some respects resembled modern Athens.

During his three weeks in Salt Lake City Burton was treated with great respect. He sampled everything permissible, talked to Mormons and Gentiles, attended Mormon services and dances, looked at prices in the stores, wandered through streets and the cemeteries, read a vast amount of Mormon and anti-Mormon literature, and interviewed Brigham Young.

A matter of particular concern to Burton—one of his reasons for visiting the Mormons in the first place—was polygamy. He was familiar with all varieties of polygamous marriages in Africa and the Near East. He had seen African chiefs with as many as 300 wives and had studied harem life among the Moslems. Mormon women were not depressed or degraded, he found; many were "exceedingly pretty and attractive" and readily accepted polygamy. He felt that as practiced by the Mormons, polygamy was puritanical, and sensuality was frowned upon.

Burton was impressed by Brigham Young. He decided that "the Prophet is no common man" and showed no evidence of bigotry, dogmatism, and fanaticism, while possessing "indomitable will and uncommon astuteness" and giving a sense of power.

In viewing the Mormon scene, Burton was as unbiased as any outside observer could have been. As his biographer, Fawn M. Brodie, remarks, "he looked at it with immense curiosity and absolutely without reproach." He defended the Mormons against slanderous stories circulated about them, although he was critical of their secularism and materialism, "mysticism and marvel-love." When he pointed out to the Mormon leaders that their religion was a combination of Jewish mysticism, millennialism, transcendentalism, and freemasonry plus certain Moslem practices, they retorted that their religion embraced all truth, regardless of source.

At the end of three weeks, Burton become bored with the quiet life of Salt Lake City and, having learned all that he could about Mormonism, went on to spend five days with the soldiers at Camp Floyd. Drinking with the American officers there he heard about, and sympathized with, their problems and compared them with those in the British Army, with which he was familiar. A few months later the American Civil War was to erupt.

After the Camp Floyd visit, Burton set out with a group of other travelers for San Francisco. The trip crossed what was considered a particularly dangerous stretch of country because of hostile Indians. "The road is full of Indians, and other scoundrels," he wrote, "but I've had my hair cropped so short that my scalp is not worth having." En route it was found that Egan's Station had been destroyed and the inhabitants massacred by Sioux Indians in revenge for the killing of some of their tribe. Three days were spent in Carson City, where Burton found far more violence and excitement than in Salt Lake City. During his short stay there, he heard of three murders. His next stop was Virginia City (two years later to be Mark Twain's home) to inspect the silver mines, and then he went on to San Francisco by way of Sacramento. Burton admired "the stirring streets, the charming faces, and delicious faces," but lingered only ten days in San Francisco before proceeding on to Panama on his way back to England.

After his visit to Salt Lake City, Burton wrote *The City of the Saints and Across the Rocky Mountains to California,* which was published in London in 1861 and became one of the classic volumes of the Old West. The American historian Allan Nevins judged that Burton was able to obtain much material on social and economic conditions that could be found nowhere else. "His attitude is scientific, his temper is tolerant, and his conclusions are in the main favorable." Another historian, H. H. Bancroft, stated that during Burton's four weeks in Salt Lake City he saw more than many men did in four years.

26. *My Diary North and South*

The outbreak of the Civil War gave British journalists a new incentive for visiting the United States. Previously correspondents had been drawn primarily to learn of such matters as new inventions, the peculiarities of the American people and their customs, democracy in action, and slavery problems.

There was a certain degree of smugness and anti-American feeling in the British reactions to the southern rebellion. The London *Morning Post,* generally regarded as the mouthpiece of Prime Minister Henry Palmerston, editorialized about the secession of the southern states: "If the Government of the United States should succeed in reannexing them . . . who can doubt that Democracy will be more aggressive, more leveling and vulgarising, if that is possible, than it ever had been before?"

The same sentiment is reflected in a report sent back by John Lothrop Motley, the American historian and diplomat:

> Nothing can exceed the virulence with which the extreme conservative party regard us, nor the delight with which they look forward to our extinction as a nation. They consider such a consummation of our civil war as the most triumphant answer which could be made to their own reform party. The hatred of the English radicals is the secret of the ferocity and brutality with which the *Times,* the *Saturday Review,* and other Tory organs of the press have poured out their insults upon America ever since the war began.

William H. Russell, characterized by Allan Nevins as "one of the greatest of all war correspondents, a writer with an unusual faculty for observation and graphic description," came to the

United States in March 1861, as a special correspondent for the London *Times*. His reputation had been established by his reports of the Crimean War for the *Times*. He remained in America until just after Lincoln's inauguration and the first battle of Bull Run. It was a crucial period. Secession had left the North confused. The press was divided between northern and southern sympathizers, and many people were unconvinced that the North had the power or the right to force the rebels to remain in the Union. The North was not yet in a warlike mood.

In Washington, New York, and elsewhere, Russell met and was well received by all the important leaders. At the time, Secretary of State William Henry Seward, not Lincoln, was regarded as the strong man of the Union cause. While in Washington, Russell was a dinner guest at the White House. His description of Lincoln's appearance as he came into the dining room was memorable: "he entered with a shambling, loose, irregular, almost unsteady gait, a tall, lank, lean man, considerably over six feet in height, with stooping shoulders, long pendulous arms, terminating in hands of extraordinary dimensions, which, however, were far exceeded in proportion by his feet. He was dressed in an ill-fitting, wrinkled suit of black, which put one in mind of an undertaker's uniform at a meeting."

Nevertheless, despite this unflattering picture of the president, Russell found such redeeming features as "the eyes dark, full, and deeply set, and penetrating, full of an expression which almost amounts to tenderness." Russell left "agreeably impressed with his shrewdness, humor, and natural sagacity." Later, his respect for Lincoln's "capacity, honesty, and plain dealing" was to grow.

Mrs. Lincoln was described as of middle age and height, plump, with plain features, manners, and appearance.

After a month in Washington, before the actual outbreak of hostilities, Russell moved South, where he found a far more belligerent spirit than among the northerners. At Norfolk, Virginia, a crowd was yelling, "Down with the Yankees! Hurrah for the Southern Confederacy!" and threatening the frigate *Cumberland*. On the Wilmington, North Carolina, dock there were piles of shot and shell identified as "anti-abolitionist pills." All along the railway in the Carolinas Russell found Confederate flags fluttering in the breeze, troops waiting for the train, and great excitement about Fort Sumter, which had just been captured by the rebels. At Charleston, the fury, hatred, and war sentiment amazed him. On Morris Island, Russell reported, "secession is the fashion here. Young ladies sing for it, old ladies pray for it; old men are ready to demonstrate it."

"The utter contempt and loathing for the venerated Stars and Stripes, the abhorrence of the very words United States, the immense hatred of the Yankees on the part of these people," observed Russell, "cannot be conceived by anyone who has not seen them. I am more satisfied than ever that the Union can never be restored as it was, and that it has gone to pieces, never to be put together again, in the old shape, at any event, by any power on earth."

The South regarded itself as unbeatable. There was also widespread belief that England would intervene on the southern side because of its dependence on southern-grown cotton—a notion on which Russell cast strong doubts.

As he proceeded farther South to Pensacola, Mobile, and New Orleans, Russell was impressed by the same intense fighting spirit and a conviction that the South must never yield to the North.

When he returned to Washington by way of the Midwest, Russell found political confusion made worse by military chaos and near panic. He was back in Washington in time to accompany the army on the way to the first battle of Bull Run in July. In a famous report, he described vividly the wild battle that followed and the rout of the federal forces.

> All the roads from Centreville for miles presented such a sight as can only be witnessed in the track of the runaways of an utterly demoralized army. Drivers flogged, lashed, spurred, and beat their horses, or leaped down and abandoned their teams, and ran by the side of the road; mounted men, servants, and men in uniform, vehicles of all sorts, commissariat wagons, thronged the narrow ways. At every shot a convulsion, as it were, seized upon the morbid mass of bones, sinew, wood, and iron, and thrilled through it giving new energy and action to its desperate efforts to get free from itself.

Russell's paper, the London *Times,* was already becoming unpopular in the North for its southern sympathies. His position had become difficult before Bull Run, but his description of that battle caused him to lose favor with Lincoln and Secretary of War Edwin Stanton. The northern press gave a different account of the retreat of the northern soldiers. Such northern editors as Greeley and Bryant tried to conceal the worst aspects of the disaster. The *Chicago Tribune* hit back: "We do not know and do not care what he [Russell] saw, or says he saw, of the fight and the flight, before we found him; but from the errors and misstatements in his narrative we should be justified in believing that he was not at the battle at all. We saw nothing of the flogging, lashing, spurring, beating, and abandoning that he so graphically describes."

Russell was refused a pass to accompany General George McClellan in the opening moves to the Peninsula. Nevins points out that he had "the distinction of being the only English traveler who had been virtually forced to leave America." In any case, he decided to return to London without allowing his editor to try to change his mind. Russell believed that his difficulties resulted "because I told the truth about Bull Run and would not bend the knee to the degraded creatures who have made the very name of a free press odious to honorable men."

Actually, Russell did not share the leaning of the London *Times* toward the southern cause. He found much to dislike about what he saw during his travels in the South. While attending a session of the Confederate Congress in Montgomery, he was disgusted to find a slave auction being held nearby, where a prime field hand was being sold at a bargain price of $1,000. He saw no merit in the southern argument that the slave was better off than the African savage. "I doubt if the aboriginal is not as civilized, in the true sense of the word, as any Negro, after three degrees of descent in servitude." He did not observe any abuse of slaves, but he was repelled by the brutish labor of women in the canefields of Louisiana, and the whole concept of slavery was abhorrent to him. Throughout the lower South, Russell noted "a reckless and violent condition of society, unfavorable to civilization, and but little hopeful for the future." He disliked slavery, southern poverty, the braggart politicians he met, and such southern traditions as the special notion of honor, dueling, quick tempers, and "the swashbuckler bravado, gallant-swaggering air of the Southern men." He was convinced that to southerners the principle of "states rights meant protection to slavery, extension of slave territory, and free trade in slave produce with the outer world." This was an impossible dream, he believed, because the world at large would not have tolerated a slave nation indefinitely.

It is a tribute to Russell's objective reporting that he became unpopular with both sides. He did not return to the United States until 1881. On the basis of his experiences at that time, he wrote a rather undistinguished book on his travels in the Far West.

27. *North America*

Anthony Trollope, son of the redoubtable Frances Trollope, author of *The Domestic Manners of the Americans,* paid his first visit to the United States in 1861, at the age of forty-six. By then he had become an established novelist and had published a number of his best known works.

Although the Civil War had erupted before his arrival in America, Trollope, unlike Edward Dicey and William Russell, did not come as a war correspondent. In the opening sentence of his *North America,* he notes, "it has been the ambition of my literary life to write a book about the United States, and I had made up my mind to visit the country with this object before the intestive troubles of the United States Government had commenced." The timing may have been a coincidence, therefore, but inevitably Trollope's narrative contains constant references to the Civil War raging during his six-months' stay. Because of the war, he was unable to travel south beyond northern Virginia and the border states of Kentucky and Missouri. His time was spent on the Eastern Seaboard, in Canada, and as far west as Iowa.

Although Trollope found much to admire, particularly in the rapidly developing Northwest, he had some sharp criticisms for the spoiled children, pampered women, hurried meals, corrupt politicians, and mendacious newspapers he observed in America. Among the specific faults in American manners and customs he pointed out were allowing children to grow old too fast and to order beefsteak, cakes, and pickles for breakfast; hurry-up meals that provided no time for a guest to linger over sherry or tea; the unhealthy look of the men, blamed on business worry and hot-air furnaces; the constant talk about money; the "rowdy" character of religion; corrupt politicians conspiring with corrupt contractors; and unethical newspapers. In the large and often magnificent American hotels, he found the clerks inattentive, "extras" too expensive, meals greasy and badly served, and he had difficulties in taking a bath. Trollope was a postal official in England, and on the basis of that experience he pointed out that there was not sufficient provision for the door-to-door delivery of mail, and he was shocked at the custom of using postal appointments as political rewards.

On the other hand, Trollope thought that of every ten men in the Old World, nine would live happier lives in the United States. He also testified that he had never found an American who did not own some books, and there were ten times as many readers of Dickens, Thackeray, Tennyson, and other popular English authors in the United States as in England. Trollope added, "I have ever admired the United States as a nation. I have loved their liberty, their prowess, their intelligence, and their progress. I have sympathized with a people who themselves had no sympathy with passive security and inaction. I have felt confidence in them, and have known, as it were, that their industry must enable them to succeed as a people, while their freedom would insure them success as a nation."

Trollope's attitude toward the North-South conflict was ambivalent. He maintained his own neutrality, although he held that southern secession was unconstitutional, Buchanan's conduct had been treasonable, and that it would have been criminal of Lincoln to have accepted the Crittenden Compromise offered to head off secession. If the South had refrained from violence, however, he believed that it would have been reasonable for the North to have allowed the slave states to withdraw from the Union. He felt that neither side deserved English support. Trollope predicted that the North would gain a partial victory, but he doubted the possibility of fully restoring the Union because the North-South differences were too fundamental.

Before beginning his travels in the principal areas of the United States other than the South, Trollope spent several weeks in

Canada and also toured Maine, Vermont, and New Hampshire. Crossing the border at Niagara, Trollope concluded, "of all the sights on this earth of ours which tourists travel to see, I am inclined to give the palm to the Falls of Niagara." A glowing description follows.

From Niagara, Trollope proceeded west to Detroit by way of a night train, during which he was introduced to "the thoroughly American institution of sleeping-cars . . . the great glory of the Americans is in their wondrous contrivances." He was little impressed by Detroit, which then had about 70,000 inhabitants, and described it as "a large well-built half finished city, lying on a convenient water way. . . . It has about it perhaps as little of intrinsic interest as any of those large western towns which I visited. It is not so pleasant as Milwaukee, nor so picturesque as St. Paul, nor so grand as Chicago, nor so civilised as Cleveland, nor so busy as Buffalo." Trollope recognized, however, Detroit's "promises of a wide and still wider prosperity," with potentialities for becoming a great commercial center.

Milwaukee, "a very pleasant town, with 45,000 population," drew favorable comments because of its attractive setting, educational level, material and intellectual well-being, lack of crowding, and no signs of poverty. As his journey continued, Trollope was delighted with the scenery along the Upper Mississippi: "Of all the river scenery that I know, that of the Upper Mississippi is by far the finest and the most continued."

The most striking sight to be seen in the Midwest, in Trollope's eyes, was the vast fields of corn and wheat he saw growing and being harvested through Iowa and Illinois. The grain market was glutted with the huge overproduction, partially because the usual southern outlet was closed by the war. "I began then to know what it was for a country to overflow with milk and honey, to burst with its own fruits, and be smothered by its own riches."

Back on the East Coast, with its cultural opportunities, Trollope attended lectures in Boston by Ralph Waldo Emerson, which he found "excellent"; by Edward Everett, who was given high marks as an orator, but whose remarks were trite and platitudinous; and by Wendell Phillips, celebrated as an impassioned advocate of abolition. Trollope observed that "the practice of 'lecturing' is quite an institution in the States," and well-known figures such as Emerson drew audiences numbering in the thousands.

On a visit to nearby Cambridge, Trollope found Harvard University smaller than he had expected. In addition to its undergraduate department, he noted there were four professional schools: law, medicine, divinity, and science. The undergraduate enrollment was about 450, and a student's essential annual expenses amounted to $249. All students were required to attend a religious service of their choice on Sundays. "A handsome library" was provided, although its collection was not as extensive as anticipated, and funds were short for additions. The university's "ugly red-brick buildings" offended Trollope, who commented, "it is almost astonishing that buildings so ugly should have been erected for such a purpose."

Trollope found much to commend about Lowell's factory system, where the employees, primarily women, were well paid, clothed, fed, cared for, and educated. "Lowell is the realization of a commercial utopia," a striking contrast to such English mill towns as Manchester.

New York City had two main defects in Trollope's opinion: "In the first place there is nothing to see; and in the second place there is no mode of getting about to see anything." Nevertheless, it was "a most interesting city," third largest in "the known world." For Trollope, "New York appears to me infinitely more American than Boston, Chicago, or Washington. Free institutions, general education, and the ascendancy of dollars are the words written on every paving stone along Fifth Avenue, down Broadway, and up Wall Street. Every man can vote and values the privilege. Every man can read, and uses the privilege. Every man worships the dollar, and is down before his shrine from morning to night." One of the principal means of transportation around the city was long omnibuses that ran on rails but were pulled by horses.

Trollope's views on the rights of women would be considered reactionary in twentieth-century America. Women's dress, fashions, and social ideas were shocking to him. He had no sympathy with their demand for equality in the working and political worlds. He was convinced, in fact, that ideas of chivalry had been carried too far and had given women exaggerated ideas about the privileges to which they were entitled. "The best right a woman has," he declared, "is the right to a husband, and that is the right to which I would recommend every young woman." He ridiculed the fashion for crinoline skirts: "The woman, as she enters drags after her a misshapen, dirty mass of battered wirework, which she calls her crinoline, and which adds as much to her grace and comfort as a log of wood does to a donkey, when tied to the animal's leg in a paddock." The way in which New York women pushed themselves into public vehicles and accepted seats without thanks to the men who offered them seemed the height of rudeness to Trollope.

Trollope praised the American educational system, whereby almost everyone learned to read and write, as making life better for the population as a whole. The question of religion was a different matter: "I feel very strongly that much of that which is evil in the structure of American politics is owing to the absence of any national religion." Trollope acknowledged, however, that the nation was "religious in its tendencies," and everyone was expected to belong to some church.

Naturally, Trollope paid an extended visit to Washington and spent time with the federal troops in Virginia, Kentucky, and Missouri. The camp at Cairo, Illinois, with its ill-equipped soldiers mired down in a sea of mud depressed him, as it had William Howard Russell. Trollope felt that the design of the national capital was grand but architecturally faulty, and that the location of the White House in the low Potomac flats was unhealthy.

The final chapters of *North America* are devoted principally to an analysis of the American system of government, the president, Congress, the courts, government finance, and the postal service. Appendixes include the Declaration of Independence, Articles of Confederation and the U.S. Constitution. Most of this material lacks originality and fresh insights and, in Allan Nevins's judgment, "can be found, in more accurate form, in any good manual of civics."

Trollope himself was somewhat apologetic about his book, concluding that "it was tedious and confused, and will hardly, I think, be of future value to those who wish to make themselves acquainted with the United States." It is true that the work's arrangement is unsatisfactory and there is too much padding, but although much of the book does not make lively reading, it has enduring value as a picture of the North and West in wartime.

In later years, Trollope made four more trips to America on post office business, but he left no written account of those visits.

28. *Six Months in the Federal States*

Edward Dicey and William Russell were the best known English journalists sent over to observe and to report on the American Civil War. There were striking differences, however, in the attitudes of the two writers toward the great conflict.

Russell, representing the anti-American, pro-southern *Times,* roused northern antagonism with his acrimonious Bull Run and other stories, and so was regarded as by the North unfriendly. By contrast, as Allan Nevins comments, Dicey's work was marked by "thoughtfulness and fairness, and especially its warm friendliness toward the North at a time when most English gentlemen and writers sympathized with the South; it made a happy impression upon American readers."

Dicey, who spent six months in America for the London *Spectator* during the first half of 1862, was clearly prejudiced in favor of the North, a stand that required some courage. There was a distinct chance at the time that Britain might help the Confederacy with arms and men as well as with recognition. Dicey's warning was clear against such an eventuality: "In the interests of humanity, in the interests of America and in the interest of England, the success of the North is a thing we ought to hope and wish for."

In the confrontation between North and South, Dicey was more keenly aware than most observers of the tremendous power of the northern side:

> You had to go away from Washington to leave the war behind you. If you went up to any high point in the city whence you could look over the surrounding country, every hillside seemed covered with camps.

The white tents caught your eye on all sides; and across the river, where the dense brushwood obscured the prospect, the great army of the Potomac stretched miles away, right up to the advanced posts of the Confederates, south of the far-famed Manassas. The numbers were so vast that it was hard to realize them. During one week fifty thousand men were embarked from Washington, and yet the town and neighborhood still swarmed with troops and camps, as it seemed, undiminished in number.

The principal reason for Dicey's deep sympathy with the federal cause was his abhorrence of slavery. Aside from the question of slavery, he believed that "the cause for which the North was fighting was the cause of freedom, of national existence, and of the world's progress." A matter relating to slavery that he was anxious to investigate was the status of free blacks in American society: "Everywhere and in all seasons the colored people form a separate community." This situation reflected the popular feeling of the free states towards the free black. Some justification existed for that sentiment, Dicey noted, for in every northern city the free Negroes were the poorest and most prone to crime of any part of the population. Dicey excused white Americans in part on the basis of historical antecedents, pointing out that, "Wherever our Anglo-Saxon race has spread itself, it has shown an uniform intolerance of an inferior race."

Dicey paid an extended visit to Washington. His observations, frequently unfavorable, are reported in a series of chapters on features of the nation's capitol; the Congress; and federal, state, and territorial constitutions. Abraham Lincoln made a strong impression on him, as is revealed in the following passage:

If you take the stock English caricature of the typical Yankee, you have the likeness of the President. To say that he is ugly is nothing, to add that his figure is grotesque is to convey no adequate impression. Fancy a man six-foot and thin out of proportion, with long bony arms and legs, which, somehow, seem to be always in the way . . . Clothe this figure, then, in a long, tight, badly-fitting suit of black, creased, soiled, and puckered up at every salient point of the figure—and every point of this figure is salient . . . add to all this an air of strength, physical as well as moral, and a strange look of dignity coupled with

all this grotesqueness, and you will have the impression left upon me
by Abraham Lincoln. You would never say that he was a gentleman;
you would still less say he was not one.

One of the opening chapters of *Six Months in the Federal States*
is devoted to a discussion of "The American Press." Provincial
newspapers were numerous, but three New York papers dominated
the field: James Gordon Bennett's *Herald,* with the largest circulation; Horace Greeley's *Tribune;* and Henry Raymond's *Times.*
Dicey's criticisms of the *Herald* were scathing; he accused it of
using blackmail against public men, lacking political principles,
and being utterly unscrupulous. The secret of its success, he
suggested, was that it was the most readable of the New York
papers, carried the fullest, if not the most accurate, news reports,
and catered to the "prejudices and vanity of the American people."
Dicey was struck by the number of newspapers published and
sold, concluding that "The American might be defined as a
newspaper-reading animal."

Although Dicey stayed in the United States only six months,
he traveled widely. He visited the West, notably Kentucky,
Tennessee, West Virginia, Missouri, and Illinois, and saw something of life on the Mississippi shortly before Mark Twain wrote
about the great river. His judgments on some of the leading
cities he visited are of interest. Cincinnati, "Queen City of the
West," had an air of "wealth, and education, and refinement"
because of its many music shops, print depots, and bookstands;
the German influence on the place and people was evident.
Nashville was rated as "the most picturesque" American city
because of its unusual setting. St. Louis, "the capital city of the
great west," was the starting point for the overland caravans
headed for the Pacific; one-tenth of all the shops there were
liquor stores. "Of all American commercial cities," remarked
Dicey, "Chicago is, to my mind, the handsomest."

Dicey liked Boston most of all, observing "putting aside the
dreary six months' winter of ice and snow, I would choose
Boston for my dwellingplace in the States. The town itself is so
bright and clean, so full of life without bustle; and then the
suburbs are such pleasant places."

While in New England, Dicey became well acquainted with the leaders of the abolition movement. One chapter of his book deals with Wendell Phillips, and another to the abolitionists in general.

Dicey was asked frequently whether he would like to live in America, and his reply was that it would depend entirely upon circumstances. He felt that the wants of a person of wealth and highly educated tastes could be more easily satisfied in the Old World. "But the man who has his living to earn is better off, in almost every respect, in America than he is in England."

Dicey admired American family life. "These reflections on American society would be imperfect," he stated, "if I said nothing as to the great charm which surrounds all family relations in the North. Compared with Europe, domestic scandals are unknown; and between parents, and their grown-up children, there exists a degree of familiarity and intimacy which one seldom witnesses in this country. If family life is the foundation of all permanent good in the social system, then, in spite of its present defects and shortcomings, the outlook for the American society of the future is a very bright one."

Dicey had considerable impact on English public opinion as editor of the *London Daily News* in 1870 and of the *London Observer* from 1871 to 1889. He was permanently affected by his American experiences.

29. *The Americans at Home*

Perhaps the most comprehensive examination of post-Civil War America came from the pen of a Scottish clergyman, David Macrae. His *The Americans at Home* was based on an extensive tour in 1867–68, immediately following the war's end.

In a "Preliminary" statement, Macrae announced that his purpose, in part, was to dispel "the old popular notion of an American as a man who wore Nankeen [from Nanking, China] trousers, carried a bowie-knife, sat with his feet on a mantelpiece, and squirted tobacco juice on the carpet."

As was a common practice among visitors from Britain, Macrae entered America by way of Canada, landing at Quebec and spending some time traveling in Upper and Lower Canada before coming to the United States.

Macrae's first impression of the States was the accelerated life-style of the people. Everyone seemed to be working under high pressure. "People are earlier astir; stores are open, streets are busier; the shops are driving a more vigorous trade; the trains and steamers and ferry-boats and horse-cars are more crowded. . . . Business is carried on more swiftly and more recklessly."

The hurried pace of living carried over into eating habits. Macrae reported that he had "seen business men in America shoot a dinner down, and to be off to work again, in the time it would take an Englishman to sharpen the carving-knife, and decide where he had better begin to cut." Six gentlemen at the Opera Restaurant in Chicago were timed. Each took an average of three and three-quarters minutes to finish their dinners.

Macrae attributed the hurry and rush of American life to three principal factors: the stimulating climate; the vastness of the country, opening up endless opportunities; and republican institutions, which place no limit on individual aspirations. "Whatever be the cause," concluded Macrae, "the fact remains that the people of the United States are the most active, pushing, and ambitious people on the face of the earth." One manifestation of such ambition was the avid desire for money-making among men, women, and even children.

Macrae found American girls, as a rule, "gentle, kind, agreeable, affectionate, and lovely to look at." He saw more signs of emancipation among women than expected: women were teachers, public lecturers, physicians, lawyers, and ministers, although it was conceded that such cases were uncommon. American girls were better educated, better informed, and more interesting conversationalists than English girls. Macrae particularly enjoyed meeting American children, whom he noted were precocious and entered readily into the family life. Somewhat offensive, however, were their tendency to pertness and lack of respect for parents. He observed that corporal punishment had practically been abolished in the schools, domestic help was increasingly unavailable and unsatisfactory, and blacks made excellent servants in homes and hotels.

Among colorful personalities Macrae met early in his travels was the celebrated minister Henry Ward Beecher, whom he heard preach several times.

Heading south, Macrae made stops in New York City, Philadelphia, Baltimore, and Washington. While in Washington, he met President Johnson, whom he described as "tall, dark-complexioned, broad-shoulders, stands erect, and has much more of dignity in his manner and appearance than I had expected to find." He also met General Grant, who was then acting as secretary of war. Macrae saw him as "a small man, with a grim little mouth, looking all the grimmer by reason of his reddish-brown moustache being cut across as with a scissors, leaving it square and bristly."

Under the guidance of the Superintendent of Education for the District of Columbia, Macrae visited the black schools of

Georgetown. Eight schools were clustered together under one roof. Each grade had its own room and teacher, and the children were well disciplined and eager to learn.

Continuing his southern route, Macrae stopped over in Richmond to find the city still in ruins from the war, but with reconstruction in progress. There he witnessed for the first time black and white members sitting together in the state legislature. In Richmond, too, he heard a speech by General Benjamin "Beast" Butler, reputed to be the most detested man in the South. As military governor of New Orleans after the end of the war, Butler was known as "Spoons" Butler because of his reputation for stealing silver. Macrae called him "unlovable," but believed that he had administrative ability of a high order and kept New Orleans clean, orderly, and healthy.

Macrae relates a number of stories about a Civil War general whom he regarded as a much more admirable figure, "Stonewall" Jackson.

At Lexington, Macrae visited Jackson's grave and went on to see Washington College (later Washington and Lee University), where Robert E. Lee was serving as president. After meeting Lee, Macrae wrote the following description of the famous general: "He is a noble-looking man, tall, straight, and soldier-like, with crisp hair turning white, short, trimmed beard, pointed at the chin, and dark imperial-looking eyes, very keen and searching."

A major problem for the South during and following the war was the deplorable condition of the emancipated slaves. Numerous voluntary organizations were attempted to save them from starvation, educate them, and fit them for their new condition. Of these agencies, whose work Macrae had an opportunity to observe, the most active and the most successful was the American Missionary Association. Under that society's sponsorship, high schools and normal schools were established, along with such chartered colleges as Hampton, Berea, Atlanta, and Fisk.

Macrae spent some weeks traveling in North Carolina. At Raleigh, he again found a convention of black and white delegates sitting in the legislature, revising the state constitution. In the course of his visit, he met and heard the most famous orator and politician of North Carolina, Zebulon Vance, wartime governor. As a Scotsman himself, Macrae was especially interested in the Scottish highlanders who had emigrated to North Carolina in large numbers. Many still spoke Gaelic.

As he proceeded South, Macrae saw and heard much about the devastation left by General Sherman's march to Atlanta. South Carolina had been hit particularly hard, because it was blamed for beginning the war. The old planters, formerly the South's aristocracy, were left ruined by the war, too poor to pay taxes on their land. Macrae reported, however, that among the numerous whites that he met, there was almost unanimous relief that slavery was a dead institution. The huge problem of assimilating millions of former slaves into the southern society was generally recognized, North and South.

Everywhere he could, Macrae talked with Confederate officers, walked with them over battlefields, and recorded their views of Lee and other commanders. The owner of a tobacco factory in Richmond, found favorable to free labor, is quoted as saying:

> I like it better than slavery. I would not go back to the slavery system if I could. Labor is cheaper now and more easily managed. Formerly you had to keep order with the rawhide. If a man was stubborn you had to whip him. You had paid $600 or $800 for him and you could not afford to let him be idle. But now, if a man is disorderly, or won't work, you tell him to take his jacket and go. Then, again in slave times you had to keep the factory going, whether you were making money or not, for the men were always on your hands.

In the course of his travels, Macrae had many illuminating chats with freed slaves. Their immediate outlook seemed to him discouraging, but in the long run he felt that the outcome of the Civil War would be beneficial to the whole nation.

Macrae began his return travels by way of New Orleans and went north on Mississippi steamers, stopping at various cities en route until he reached Chicago. The varied wonders of the "Lightning City," Chicago, impressed him. He reached the next major stop, Boston, by train from Chicago. Memorable personalities whom Macrae was eager to meet abounded in the "Hub" city: Theodore Parker, Wendell Phillips, Horace Greeley, Rufus Choate, Ralph Waldo Emerson, Charles Sumner, Daniel Webster,

H. W. Longfellow, James Russell Lowell, and Oliver Wendell Holmes.

Macrae visited Longfellow in his home and dined informally there. The poet, he wrote, "looked older and more venerable than I had expected to find him—his long clustering hair and shaggy beard white as snow. I was struck, too, with a look of latent sadness in his eyes—an expression that vanishes at times when he is moved to laughter, but steals back into the thoughtful eye and into every line of the face, as soon as the passing thought is gone." He was less impressed by Lowell, whom he visited in his Harvard classroom and described as an "undersized gentleman . . . in plain, shooting coat and light-speckled necktie; long curling brown hair, parted in the middle, . . . began his lecture without ceremony . . . and enlivened his lecture with continual sallies of wit." Another distinguished member of the faculty was Oliver Wendell Holmes, whose opening lecture in the Harvard Medical School was heard by Macrae. Emerson and Louis Agassiz were also present. "Holmes is a plain little dapper man, his short hair brushed down like a boy's, but turning gray now . . . a powerful jaw, and a thick strong under lip that gives decision to his look, with a dash of pertness. . . . He enlivens his lecture with numerous jokes and bullet sallies of wit." Macrae's description of Ralph Waldo Emerson was equally graphic: "He has the queerest New England face, with thin features, prominent hatchet nose, and a smile of childlike sweetness and simplicity arching the face . . . a gaunt, long-limbed man, dressed in a high collared surtout. . . . Eyes full of sparkling geniality."

In the concluding chapters of *The Americans at Home,* Macrae offers observations on a variety of matters, primarily relating to New England. He found evidence of universal comfort and prosperity all through that region. The men of New England "swear less, drink less, chew less" than people of the South and West. Weddings and funerals were frequently elaborate and expensive. Saloons and bars were everywhere, and more drinking took place in these than in homes. Liquor laws were observed only to the extent that they were favored and supported by people generally.

Macrae called America "a world of newspapers . . . and half the life of an American." More daily newspapers were published in New York State than all England, Scotland, and Ireland combined. The most widely read were three New York journals: *Tribune, Herald,* and *World.* The *New York Times* was another influential newspaper.

"Nothing in America excited my admiration more than the system of common schools," Macrae declared. He approved of having the system being supported by a school tax imposed by the people upon themselves. In many communities, grammar and high schools, also free, were added. To make the plan fully effective, in Macrae's opinion, compulsory attendance laws were needed. The great mass of American children were educated in the common schools, although numerous private academies were supported by people "afraid to let their own children commingle with other children." At the time of Macrae's investigation, the question of whether boys and girls should be educated separately was determined by each district for itself. He thought that the presence of girls had a refining influence on the males. Oberlin College, one of the first coeducational institutions, "was the only college in which I saw no spittoons, and nobody using tobacco." Macrae favored the separation of secular and religious education.

Shortly before his death, Macrae made a return visit to the United States. His *America Revisited* was published in Glasgow in 1908.

30. *The American Commonwealth*

During the 1860s and 70s there was widespread agitation in Europe for greater republicanism in government. The American republic was a prime example for those who wished to study practical applications of democratic principles. How could democracy be reconciled with the need for public order and some form of authority in government?

Among those interested in these questions was a young Scot named James Bryce, who had made a brilliant record as an Oxford University student. In 1870, Bryce and a close friend, Albert Venn Dicey, decided to visit the United States to study its constitutional government. Bryce was then age thirty-two; he was in fine physical condition, toughened by walking tours in the Alps and in his native Scotland. According to the journal he kept of his American travels, he enjoyed many early morning baths in cold mountain streams and lakes while traveling through the White Mountains in New Hampshire on his way to the Midwest and up the Mississippi to Minneapolis. In Boston, he met Longfellow and Oliver Wendell Holmes, Jr.; the latter became a lifelong friend.

Bryce went by train to Chicago, where he studied the coeducational system, the success of which persuaded him to work for the education of women in Britain. He and Dicey agreed that "Chicago is the handsomest city we have seen in America. You feel that those who have built the city have felt it was becoming great, and have been inspired by this spirit to do their best."

Bryce saw an unattractive aspect of American political life

when he attended a Democratic party convention in New York that was dominated by Boss Tweed, soon to be indicted for graft, embezzlement, and plunder on a grand scale.

Bryce thus had mixed impressions of America when he returned to England after several months, although on the whole his views were favorable. He liked the easy social relationships, the lack of barriers between social classes, and the lack of rigid hierarchies in the United States.

Bryce's second tour came eleven years later, in 1881. His itinerary took him by train west through Kansas to Colorado and Utah, through Salt Lake City to San Francisco, north to Oregon, and then back to St. Louis, Kentucky, Tennessee, and Georgia to Washington. He remarked on the monotony in appearance of American cities, all so similar in planning.

Back home in England, Bryce was gaining distinction as a political leader, a member of Parliament starting in 1880, and one of the heads of the Liberal party. Among the important offices he held was Under-Secretary of State for Foreign Affairs. His career in British politics ended with his appointment as Ambassador to the United States, a position he held until 1913.

During his first contacts with the United States, Bryce conceived the idea of a major work on American democracy. He had previously written articles on American life for English journals, but now he planned a detailed treatise to explore every side of the social and political organization of American government. During a third trip in 1883, he collected relevant materials and discussed the project with a variety of government officials and other knowledgable individuals. The first edition of Bryce's monumental *The American Commonwealth,* in two volumes, came off the press in 1888. It was quickly recognized as a masterpiece.

The American Commonwealth ranks second only to Tocqueville's *Democracy in America* in its deep understanding of American political philosophy, and probably is second to none as a systematic analysis and interpretation of American government. For nearly a century, the book has served as a basic text for the study of political science as applied to America.

Woodrow Wilson pointed out in reviewing the first edition of *The American Commonwealth* that Bryce brought extraordinary qualifications to his task of studying the complexities of American government. "He has breathed the air of practical politics in the country from which we get our habits of political action," Wilson wrote, "and he is so familiar with the machinery of government at home as to be able to perceive at once the most characteristic differences as well as the real resemblances, between political arrangements in England and in the United States." Bryce was also schooled in ancient Roman law and English legal practice and possessed a broad knowledge of comparative politics. To these qualities he added an intimate acquaintance with American affairs based on his several extended visits and study and a warm sympathy with American ways of life.

The American Commonwealth is divided into six parts. The least original part of the work, because it has been dealt with by numerous commentators, is titled "The National Government." Bryce provided fresh insight, however, as he examined both legal theory and interpretation and the practical aspects and operation of the federal machinery. Congress, the presidency, and the federal courts are discussed from practically every conceivable point of view. The most striking difference between the American and all other governments of the world, Bryce found, is the separation of the executive and legislative functions. Everywhere else the legislature is provided with ministerial leadership or cabinet government in some form. The third element in the system of checks and balances created by the Founding Fathers is, of course, an independent judiciary.

Bryce stressed the uniqueness of the American Constitution in his opening sentence: "The acceptance of the Constitution made the American people a nation"; and further, "the subjection of all the ordinary authorities and organs of government to a supreme instrument expressing the will of the sovereign people, and capable of being altered by them only, has been usually deemed the most remarkable novelty of the American system."

Bryce questioned whether America always chooses its ablest men for the presidency: "Europeans often ask, and Americans do not always explain, how it happens that the office of President of the United States, the greatest in the world . . . is not more frequently filled by great and striking men. In America, which is beyond all other countries, the country of a 'career open to talents,' a country, moreover, in which political life is unusually keen and political ambition widely diffused, it might be expected that the highest place would always be won by a man of brilliant gifts."

The explanations Bryce offered are that the proportion of first-rate ability drawn into politics is smaller in America than in most European countries (Tocqueville likewise pointed out the difficulties in recruiting men of superior ability for public office); the methods and habits of Congress and of political life generally give fewer opportunities for personal distinction; and eminent men make more enemies than do obscure individuals. Certainly Bryce was mistaken in any blanket condemnation of the quality of men who have attained the presidency, but unquestionably a high proportion of those who have occupied the White House has been mediocre.

Bryce expressed himself on two frequently debated issues relating to the presidency. He questioned the wisdom of an election by popular vote: "To have left the choice of the chief magistrate to a direct popular vote over the whole country would have raised a dangerous excitement, and would have given too much encouragement to candidates of merely popular gifts." He also criticized the perils of the casual method by which vice-presidents are usually selected, for "if the president happens to die, a man of small account may step into the chief magistracy of the nation." In actual practice, Bryce conceded that the electoral college system is ordinarily an election of the president by a majority of the popular vote, even though indirect, but the system may occasionally result in the president's being elected by a minority of popular votes.

The control over foreign policy exercised by the Senate has both advantages and disadvantages, in Bryce's view. The Senate "may deal with foreign policy in a narrow, sectional, electioneering spirit indifferent to foreign affairs," but the system "has tended, by discouraging the executive from schemes which may prove resultless, to diminish the taste for foreign enterprises, and to save the country from being entangled with alliances, protectorates, responsibilities of all sorts beyond its own frontiers"—a conclusion of doubtful validity in the light of recent history.

The senatorial function of confirming nominations submitted by the president is often abused in practice, in Bryce's opinion, as "Senators have used their right of confirmation to secure for themselves a huge mass of federal patronage . . . by means of this right, a majority hostile to the president can thwart and annoy him."

Concerning the House of Representatives, Bryce saw serious drawbacks in the frequent elections and high rate of turnover in its membership. "Uneasy lies the head of an ambitious Congressman," he observed, "for the chances are about even that he will lose his seat at the next election. Anyone can see how much influence this constant change in the composition of the American House must have upon its legislative efficiency."

In a series of chapters, largely descriptive but sometimes critical and interpretive, Bryce considered in detail the Senate as an executive and judicial body, the work and committees of the House, congressional legislation and finance, the relations of the two houses, and the relation of Congress to the president. Next he reviewed the federal courts, including the Supreme Court and the circuit and district courts, and their relationships to the state courts.

"This complex system of two jurisdictions (Federal and State) over the whole country," Bryce found "after a hundred and twenty years of experience, despite the wonder of foreigners, works smoothly." The lack of conflict results from the principle that federal law must prevail wherever applicable. Bryce admired the Supreme Court as "the living voice of the Constitution." He noted its responsiveness to the will of the people: "The Supreme Court feels the touch of public opinion. Opinion is stronger in America than anywhere else in the world, and judges are only men. To yield a little may be prudent, for the tree that cannot bend to the blast may be broken." Another characteristic is that the Court's temper and tendencies vary "according to the political proclivities of the men who composed it," although the changes are slow.

In the light of Franklin Delano Roosevelt's attempt years later to enlarge the Court, it is of interest to recall Bryce's comments.

He observed that the number of judges in the Supreme Court is unspecified. "Here was a weak point, a joint in the Court's armor through which a weapon might some day penetrate. As the Constitution does not prescribe the number of justices, a statute may increase or diminish the number as Congress thinks fit, and it is possible the court might be 'packed' for a purpose."

Bryce was the first major writer on political science to treat comprehensively the history, nature, course of development, and operations of state and local government. Earlier commentators had concentrated on the federal system. Bryce considered the state constitutions to be "a mine of instruction for the natural history of democratic institutions," because they are more frequently amended, generally longer, and more filled with minute matters than is the federal Constitution. As Woodrow Wilson remarked, "The states have been laboratories in which English habits, English law, English political principles have been put to the most varied, and sometimes to the most curious, tests; and it is by the variations of institutions under differing circumstances that the nature and laws of institutional growth are to be learned."

With a few exceptions, Bryce was struck by the lack of power of state governors, although in older states and during times of crises they still had great influence. Most governmental authority resided in the state legislatures, which Bryce was convinced were even more deficient than the Congress in able and high-minded men among their members. In general, it was his conclusion that "the dignity and magnitude of state politics have declined" as the power of the national government expanded.

Reminiscent of Lincoln Steffens's muckraking work, *The Shame of the Cities,* is Bryce's criticism of municipal government:

> There is no denying that the government of cities is the one conspicuous failure of the United States. The deficiencies of the national government tell but little for evil on the welfare of the people. The faults of the State governments are insignificant compared with the extravagance, corruption, and mismanagement which mark the administrations of most of the great cities. For these evils are not confined to one or two cities. . . . Even in cities of the third rank similar phenomena may occasionally be discerned.

The plight of municipal government has become more aggravated rather than diminished since Bryce's day, of course, although corruption is probably much less prevalent. Pessimists have even concluded that the largest cities are ungovernable from a practical standpoint, and their complex problems virtually insoluble.

"The Party System," the third major part of *The American Commonwealth,* is analyzed in systematic detail. Bryce described the political machine and the political bosses and the methods of practical politics; sketched party history and the main characteristics of the leading parties; and discussed the conditions of public life that tend to keep the best men out of politics and to produce certain distinctively American types of politicians. He also studied in depth the inner workings of nominating conventions; this mechanism had grown up, according to Bryce, as "an effort of nature to fill the void left in America by the absence of the European parliamentary or cabinet system, under which an executive is called into being out of the legislature by the majority of the legislature. In the European system no single act of nomination is necessary, because the leader of the majority comes gradually to the top in virtue of his own strength."

The highly significant role of public opinion in American politics and public affairs in general impressed Bryce. "Of all the experiments which America has made," he declared, "public opinion is that which best deserves study, for she has shown more boldness in trusting it, in recognizing and giving effect to it, than has yet been shown elsewhere." This is true, Bryce observed, despite the fact that the Founding Fathers who invented the machinery of checks and balances in government "were anxious not so much to develop public opinion as to resist and build up breakwaters against it," because "they were penetrated by a sense of the dangers incident to democracy." Also of great importance in Bryce's view is that public opinion in the United States "is the opinion of the whole nation, with little distinction of social classes."

In his final section, "Social Institutions," Bryce dealt with railroads, Wall Street, the bench, the bar, the universities, the influence of religion, the position of women, the influence of democracy on thought and on creative intellectual power, American oratory, and concluded with some forecasts of the political, social, and economic future of the United States.

Bryce shared many of Tocqueville's views regarding the strength and weaknesses of American democracy. He admired the national acceptance of law and legal methods, restrictions on official authority, and the people's faith in liberty and in their own institutions. In describing democracy's weaknesses, he again followed Tocqueville in a number of important aspects. His chief criticisms concern the general level of political life in America, the low intellectual standard of leadership, and the inefficiency of government. Bryce found a lack of dignity among the people's representatives, who "behave as ordinary men," and a lack of knowledge and judgment in legislative and administrative affairs. The best talent is not attracted to public life, consequently all branches of government function below the level to be expected in a great nation.

Bryce points out two defects of American democracy that were less observable when Tocqueville was writing in the 1830s: the corrupt and unethical practices prevalent in party politics and in city governments and the tremendous power of wealth in America. The political machines, rings, and bosses are condemned as "the ugliest feature" in American politics. Civil service reform and better ballot and election laws, Bryce thought, would help to correct the weaknesses that had grown up over a period of years.

Bryce was convinced that American democracy was strong enough to overcome any forces of evil that might menace it. Near the end of his life (he died in 1922) he wrote: "No Englishman who remembers American politics as they were half a century ago, and who, having lived in the United States, has formed an affection as well as an admiration for its people will fail to rejoice at the many signs that the sense of public duty has grown stronger, that the standards of public life are steadily rising, that democracy is more and more showing itself a force making for ordered progress, true to the principles of Liberty and Equality from which it sprang."

As ambassador, Bryce proved to be a skilled diplomat, his mission aided by personal friendships with Presidents Theodore Roosevelt, William Howard Taft, and Wilson. When he returned to England in 1913, he was knighted in recognition of his services. Wilson continued to seek his advice during World War I. Bryce felt strongly that the wealth and power of the New World would be needed to correct the problems of the Old World. America had obligations, he believed, to accept the responsibilities that came with power, rather than retreating into isolationism.

31. *The Southern States since the War, 1870–71*

The large influx of foreign travelers in the United States dwindled sharply during and immediately after the Civil War. An exception is Robert Somers, whose *The Southern States since the War* was rated by Allan Nevins as "The most valuable of all British books of travel dealing with the Reconstruction era . . . a painstaking and impartial work, not to be neglected."

Somers, a native of Scotland, had an impressive career as an author and journalist before coming to America in 1870. He had written books on education, labor, banking, and commercial questions, and had an established reputation as an economist. His primary concern when he landed in America was to study the South, where the whole way of life had been so lately wracked by war. It appears that he had been a southern sympathizer during the war. If so, as an observer he subordinated such sympathy and gave a fair, detached, and balanced appraisal of the region's economic life, politics, and race relations. He was particularly interested in economic and social matters: cotton and sugar culture, blacks, railroads, natural resources, labor, industry, immigration, and education.

Somers's written observations began and ended in Washington, D.C., over a five-month period, 1870–71, during which he covered thousands of miles by all kinds of conveyances. His route took him through Virginia, North and South Carolina, Georgia, Tennessee, Alabama, Mississippi, and Louisiana to New Orleans, and back by way of Arkansas, Kentucky, Ohio, Tennessee, and Washington, to return home.

The overwhelming problem Somers encountered throughout the South was what to do with four million newly freed blacks. Vast readjustments were required to fit them back into southern society. A system of wages and sharing of crops had to be agreed upon, grants of land made, schools provided, and political rights assured. A majority of cotton, tobacco, and rice farmers still considered black labor indispensable. In the course of his travels, Somers found the South struggling with these and many related questions.

A common school system had existed in the South before the Civil War, free to all white children. The addition of black children demanded more school buildings, more teachers, more administrators, and increased expenditures of every kind. Qualified teachers were scarce. In some areas, such as New Orleans, private schools were being set up to fill the gap. Separate schools for white and black children were the prevailing plan.

The political power of the blacks, lead by carpetbaggers and "scallawags," was exerted early. In North Carolina, a corrupt state government under Governor Holden was kept in power by manipulating the black vote. A test oath excluded from office persons who had taken part in the war. In South Carolina, the legislature was composed of 91 blacks and 64 white men. The white people of the state were thus practically disfranchised. On every hand there were charges of misgovernment, extravagant expenditures, jobbery, and corruption. Blacks voted preponderantly Republican, because that party had given them freedom and guaranteed them certain rights under the Reconstruction.

A backlash had naturally developed as whites attempted to regain political power. A secret society, the Ku Klux Klan, was organized and spread rapidly over the South soon after the close of the war, spreading alarm among federal soldiers and blacks. By the time Somers was writing, he found that "the institution is dying fast," although he expected that "it is the deep vice of all such secret societies to survive, in a more degenerate form," a well-founded prophecy.

The importance of agricultural reform was being recognized by many southern farmers. Much land had been depleted by lack of crop rotation, shallow plowing, and insufficient fertilizer. The farmers' yields were being greatly increased by the use of guano or phosphates, selected seed, and better methods of cultivation. Agricultural societies and farm journals were helping to spread useful information. Somers was struck by the absence of livestock on the plantations or about the farmhouses. Few cattle were visible, although wild hogs roaming through the woods were fairly common. The shortage of livestock was blamed on the war, during which nearly all cattle had been consumed, and there had not been time to replenish the herds and flocks. The absence of good grassland was also a factor in the scarcity.

The poor quality of goods available in stores appalled Somers. The worst, apparently, was whisky, described as "a dreary drug, in which there was little or no whisky, producing only vertigo, and ending in all forms of violent disorder." The bad whisky in the stores was accompanied by "bad salt, bad knives and forks, bad boots and shoes, and all the varieties of 'shoddy,' the inferior quality of which is only surpassed by their enormity of price." Somers also noted that "the sale of quack medicines has attained a magnitude to be found nowhere else," eventually ruining the health of those who become addicted to them.

One product, however, of which Somers approved, and which must have done much to ameliorate life in tropical New Orleans, was an ice factory, where 73 tons of ice a day were manufactured from distilled Mississippi water by fire and steam power.

Somers visited the principal southern cities. Richmond, former capital of the Confederacy, was "a busy and spirited town," but made no strong impression on the traveler. Charleston, thoroughly devastated by the war, was making a slow recovery. Savannah, too, had suffered severe war damage, but the "Forest City" retained much of its traditional beauty. Atlanta had achieved a remarkable rise from the ashes of war. Other leading southern cities—such as Montgomery, Mobile, and Chattanooga—were growing rapidly in population, trade, and industry and giving signs of future prosperity. In Memphis, Somers met Jefferson Davis, now an insurance company head, but still a popular figure despite his failed leadership. Added stops were made in Nashville, Louisville, and Cincinnati before Somers returned to Washington on March 20, 1871, and then returned to England.

32. *A Lady's Life in the Rocky Mountains*

According to popular tradition, the Old West was the exclusive domain of gunslingers, cowboys, trappers, desperados, and refugees from the law. As Isabella Bird Bishop wrote, it was "no region for tourists and women," but she proved otherwise.

Isabella Bird (later Mrs. John Bishop) was the daughter of an English clergyman. Her first trip abroad was made at age twenty-one. During the next fifty years she became one of the outstanding travelers of her time and author of about a dozen excellent published accounts of her expeditions. Beginning in 1854, she took a trip to America for her health. Thereafter, she circled the earth three times, usually traveling alone and staying in such places as the upper Yangtze, the Malay jungle, Tibet, Persia, Japan, Hawaii, Canada, New Zealand, Korea, and Morocco. She was a small, soft-spoken, and unassuming person of deep religious convictions. At the same time, she was an extraordinarily dedicated traveler and a skillful horsewoman capable of enduring all kinds of hardships. On the basis of her accomplishments, she was the first woman elected to the Royal Geographical Society.

The beginning of Bishop's story of *A Lady's Life in the Rocky Mountains* dates from 1872. After several visits to Australia, New Zealand, and Hawaii, she sailed for America and spent several months in a San Francisco sanatorium. In the autumn of 1873, she went by train from San Francisco into the Sierra Nevada, and then set out on a four-month, 800-mile trip through the Rockies.

181

Long letters to her sister, later collected in book form, provide picturesque glimpses of frontier towns, the lives of the settlers, and many exciting events.

Bishop frequently grew rhapsodic about the Rocky Mountain scenery, which, she wrote, "satisfies my soul . . . it exceeds the dream of my childhood. It is magnificent, and the air is life giving." Estes Park, she thought, combined the beauties of it all: "Grandeur and sublimity, not softness, are the features of Estes Park." Wildflowers bloomed in profusion: "dandelions, buttercups, larkspurs, harebells, violets, roses, blue gentian, columbine, painter's brush, and fifty others, blue and yellow predominating."

Animal life was no less plentiful. Around Lake Tahoe, Bishop found "hordes of grizzlies, brown bears, wolves, elk, deer, chipmunks, martens, minks, skunks, foxes, squirrels, and snakes." On the plains around Fort Collins there were herds of wild horses, buffalo, deer, and antelope, and in the nearby mountains, bears, mountain lions, bison, and mountain sheep. It was a hunter's paradise, and nearly everyone carried a rifle. Bishop most dreaded the reptiles. "My life is embittered by the abundance of these reptiles—rattlesnakes and moccasin snakes, both deadly, carpet snakes and green racers, reputed dangerous, water snakes, tree snakes, and mouse snakes, harmless but abominable. Seven rattlesnakes have been killed just outside the cabin since I came."

On the plains near Fort Collins, she was intrigued by prairie dog villages, with hundreds of burrows placed together and sometimes shared by owls and rattlesnakes. "The appearance of hundreds of these creatures, each eighteen inches long, sitting like dogs begging, with their paws down and all turned sunwards, is most grotesque."

Swarms of black flies polluting the food and myriads of crawling insects were a great pest in Colorado. "The bugs come out of the earth, infest the wooden walls, and cannot be got rid of by any amount of cleanliness."

Bishop was critical of most of the primitive frontier towns she visited. In Cheyenne, for example, "the roads resound with atrocious profanity," and rowdyism prevailed in the barrooms. "It is utterly slovenly-looking and unornamental, abounds in slouching bar-room-looking characters, and looks a place of low, mean lives." In Truckee, "at the height of its evening revelries—fires blazing out of doors, bar-rooms and saloons crammed, lights glaring, gaming tables thronged, fiddle and banjo in frightful discord, and the air ringing with ribaldry and profanity." In Golden City, "brick, pine, and log houses are huddled together, every other house is a saloon, and hardly a woman is to be seen." In Utah, Bishop admired Mormon industry, but described Mormon women as "ugly, and their shapeless blue dresses hideous." Boulder was "a hideous collection of frame houses on the burning plain, but it aspires to be a 'city' in virtue of being a 'distributing point' for the settlements up the Boulder Canyon, and of the discovery of a coal seam."

Crime in the frontier communities, she found, was often dealt with in rough and ready fashion. When rowdies and desperados began reigns of terror with their murders, stabbings, and shootings, vigilante committees were formed, the culprits were warned to leave town, and some of the worst were hung. In a single fortnight, an incredible number of ruffians were lynched in Cheyenne. "Nearly all the shooting affrays," Bishop reported, "arise from the most trivial causes in saloons or bar-rooms." There was considerable popular support for prohibition of liquor. "In Colorado," she noted, "whiskey is significant of all evil and violence and is the cause of most of the shooting affrays in the mining camps." Greeley, Colorado, where liquor was prohibited, was practically free of crime.

Bishop encountered numerous colorful characters. Most memorable was a notorious desperado, one-eyed Mountain Jim, who lived in a rude log cabin that "looked like the den of a wild animal." As described, he was "a broad, thickset man of middle height, wearing a grey hunting suit much the worse for wear, a digger's scarf knotted round his waist, a knife in his belt, and a revolver sticking out of the breast pocket of his coat." His behavior belied his appearance, however, for he impressed Bishop as having "the manner of a chivalrous gentleman, his accent refined, and his language easy and elegant." Mountain Jim was one of the famous scouts of the plains, the hero of many daring exploits, but a dangerous man when drunk.

Hardly less famous was Comanche Bill, who accompanied

Bishop through Hall's Gulch, Colorado. Although she found him to be an intelligent, courteous companion, he "was one of the most notorious desperados of the Rocky Mountains, and the greatest Indian exterminator on the frontier," ever seeking revenge for the massacre of his family by Indians.

More appealing was a Welchman, Evans, who operated cabins at Estes Park and was described as "short and small, hospitable, careless, reckless, jolly, social, convivial, peppery, good natured," and also, "a splendid shot, an expert and successful hunter, a bold mountaineer, a good rider, a capital cook."

At Truckee, Bishop wanted to hire a horse, and a man came in from the bar to supply her. "This man, the very type a western pioneer," she wrote, "bowed, threw himself into a rocking-chair, drew a spitoon beside him, cut a fresh quid of tobacco, began to chew energetically, and put his feet, cased in miry high boots, into which his trousers were tucked, on the top of the stove."

Everywhere Bishop went, women were treated in exemplary fashion. "Womanly dignity and manly respect for women are the salt of society in this wild West," she found. "The habit of respectful courtesy to women prevailed in that region."

Bishop's few contacts with Indians left her depressed and with little hope for their future. An encampment of about 500 Utes near Denver was described as "a disorderly and dirty huddle of lodges, ponies, men, squaws, children, skins, bones, and raw meat." The government's treatment of the Indians, in her view, "reduces them to a degraded pauperism, devoid of the very first elements of civilization," while the "Indian agency has been a sink of fraud and corruption."

A surprisingly high percentage of the residents of the Rocky Mountain region were there for health reasons, most often tuberculosis. As Bishop noted, "the climate of Colorado is considered the finest in North America, and consumptives, asthmatics, dyspeptics, and sufferers from nervous diseases, are here in hundreds and thousands, either trying the 'camp cure' for three or four months, or settling here permanently."

Bishop's most spectacular exploit in the Rockies was the ascent of Long's Peak, 14,700 feet high, which had been climbed for the first time only five years previously. This "American Matterhorn" dwarfed all the surrounding mountains and generated strong winds, thunder, and lightning. Mountain Jim agreed to serve as guide, and they reached the summit after an exceedingly exhausting and hazardous two-day climb. Without Jim, it would have been impossible; he "dragged me up, like a bale of goods, by sheer force of muscle," Bishop confessed. Nevertheless, she concluded, "a more successful ascent of the Peak was never made, and I would not now exchange my memories of its perfect beauty and extraordinary sublimity for any other experience of mountaineering in any part of the world."

Bishop's stay in the Rockies lasted from early September to mid-December 1873. A drive of several hours over the plains brought her to Greeley, "and a few hours later, in the far blue distance, the Rocky Mountains, and all that they enclose, went down below the prairie sea." Thus ended her Rocky Mountain adventure.

After returning to Great Britain, Bishop continued her career as a world traveler: She spent seven months traveling in the interior of Japan, five months in the Malay Peninsula, and established hospitals in Kashmir, the Punjab, China, and Korea. In her mid-sixties, she again toured Canada, Japan, Korea, and China. As Daniel Boorstin commented, "It is hard to recall another woman in any age or country who traveled so widely, who saw so much, and who left so perceptive a record of what she saw. There was nothing faddish or snobbish, and very little that was romantic in her travel interests."

33. *Wanderings in the Western Land*

After the Civil War, travel west of the Mississippi and on to the West Coast became popular. It held a particular attraction for sportsmen and hunters because of the variety and prolificacy of wildlife in the West. Like other travelers, the sportsmen frequently published accounts of their experiences. As early as 1804, François André Michaux wrote that "the inhabitants along the Ohio employ the greatest part of their time in deer and bear hunting, for the sake of the skins which they sell." A British member of Parliament, Sir G. C. G. F. Berkeley, who was chiefly interested in hunting on the western plains, spent four months in the United States, wrote *English Sportsman in Western Prairies* in 1861, and urged his colleagues to take a similar trip as a vacation between Parliamentary sessions. A later example is Horace Vachell's 1901 *Life and Sport on the Pacific Slope,* an excellent account of ranching, fishing, and hunting in California by the English novelist.

Falling between the latter two chronologically is A. P. Vivian's 1879 *Wanderings in the Western Land,* a narrative of big-game hunting in the Rockies, the scenery of the Yosemite and other regions, and mining in Utah and Nevada.

Vivian, a member of Parliament, landed at St. John's, Newfoundland, in August 1877. During the weeks that followed, he traveled to Halifax, Quebec, Montreal, Toronto, and other localities in southern Canada, then to Niagara. Before leaving Canada, he was given a taste of hunting bears and moose, but serious big-game hunting did not begin until he reached the Rockies in October.

En route west, Vivian recorded impressions of several American cities. He described Chicago, then with a population of about 400,000, as "that marvel of modern cities, and truly it is a marvel when we consider that it is only six years ago since it was almost destroyed by fire." Rebuilding had been so rapid and successful, "it is superior in every way to what it was before the terrible disaster."

Vivian wrote admiringly of the tremendous accomplishments of the Union Pacific and Central Pacific Companies in constructing the railroad from Chicago to San Francisco while confronted by hostile Indians, great engineering difficulties, transportation of expensive materials for long distances, dependence on an army of toughs and desperados as a work force, and logistics of feeding and supplying these crews.

After train service was finally in operation, Vivian recounted a wild tale of a train robbery by six masked ruffians. About a fortnight before he rode the Union Pacific west, an express train bound eastward was stopped 361 miles west of Omaha at Big Springs, and gold valued at $60,000, together with the passengers' personal valuables, was taken. The desperados rode off into the night. Three were later shot and killed by sheriffs, but the others escaped.

The area between Omaha and Cheyenne, where the buffalo formerly roamed in countless numbers, was now filled with huge herds of cattle. As many as ten thousand cattle might bear the brand of the same stockowner. Most were shipped by rail to Chicago. "These vast, monotonous bare-looking prairies are already the great beef-producing regions of the United States."

Vivian came to admire "cow punchers" or cowboys, finding them honest and straightforward in their dealings, always good humored and ready to assist travelers, although he was appalled by their "fearful swearing." The same addiction to profanity was characteristic of miners and a majority of other westerners.

Vivian's introduction to the Rocky Mountain wildlife was fairly tame. He was intrigued by prairie dog colonies. These cheery little animals, he thought, helped to break the monotony of a long journey, providing interest in an "often monotonous lifeless landscape."

His next encounter was considerably less agreeable. A cabin at Estes Park in which Vivian and his party had planned to stay had been invaded by a family of skunks. The beasts resented attempts to force them out and made the place completely uninhabitable with their fearful smell. Hunting dogs, learning from experience, dared not attack them.

The first success in going after big game came with the shooting of a four-year-old "range" grizzly bear. Because of difficulties in procuring food at high altitudes, this type of bear did not reach great size, but had much thicker and warmer hides than did grizzlies that inhabited lower altitudes.

At Fort Collins, then a small village, Vivian met a famous hunter, Jim Baker, who lived on Snake River with his Indian wife and a large family. Baker was noted for his skill in trapping beavers, "by any boat he may choose," in localities where other hunters found none.

Pronghorn antelopes abounded in the area where Vivian hunted. Their powers of sight and smell were acute, and they were swift runners over short distances. They were relatively small, with the males weighing up to 120 pounds. The herds migrated for long distances according to the season of the year, and frequented the open plains instead of heavy-timbered districts. Only the males grew horns.

Vivian caught glimpses of the grey timber wolf, although he was never close enough to shoot one. These were "very powerful, but at the same time cowardly and suspicious animals," about four or five feet in length and as tall as deerhounds. The timber wolf generally traveled alone, unlike the smaller coyotes that were often seen in small packs. Vivian was struck by "the coyote's unearthly barking and yelling," which went on night after night.

A smaller, extremely "pugnacious little animal" was the wolverine, which Vivian's party observed although rarely spotted except in the most mountainous areas. Equipped with formidable claws, the wolverine was reported to be so ferocious that it was a match for a small bear.

Prepared to defend itself with another type of weapon was the porcupine, common in the Rocky Mountain region. No hunting dog exposed to a skunk's vile odor or to a porcupine's sharp quills ever risked another encounter. Vivian spent hours extracting quills from his favorite dog Ned, which had to learn the hard way.

A big game animal sought by Vivian was the elk, or wapiti. He first became aware of this large member of the deer family when he heard the strange roaring, or rather whistling, of a huge bull elk. He described it as "weird, wild and peculiar," a sound that did not seem to fit "so colossal an animal." One herd he saw included about thirty elk, twenty-five cows and five stags, dominated by a master stag.

A treasured prize of Vivian's hunting expedition was a magnificent male mountain lion that measured eight feet six inches from nose to tip of tail, weighed about 150 pounds, and had a beautiful skin.

For the most part, Vivian and his fellow hunters lived off the land, their food consisting primarily of prime venison from antelope and elk supplemented by much less tasty sage hens and jack rabbits. The sage hens were magnificent birds; males measured as much as two-and-a-half feet in length and weighed up to six pounds.

Another animal Vivian was ambitious to take was a mountain sheep, already becoming rare. He was unsuccessful, however, and failed to obtain a specimen of the "half-sheep half-deer."

Near the end of his stay in the Rockies, Vivian was able to fulfill another ambition: to go on a buffalo hunt. He spotted great herds of bison, some of them numbering in the hundreds. Vivian was highly critical of "the miserable and wanton destruction of this fine beast," and predicted that lacking government protection, it would soon become extinct.

Vivian's stay in the Rockies was in late fall and winter, and survival required extraordinary courage, fortitude, and stamina. He commented often on snowstorms, deep snows, sub-zero temperatures, and rough country. On several occasions he risked death by freezing, being lost on unfamiliar mountain trails, or other perils.

For the record, Vivian totaled the animals killed during his hunting tour: one moose, one caribou, four bull buffalos, nine elk, three deer, ten antelopes, one puma, and one bear.

After his hunting trip, Vivian proceeded west, stopping first in Nevada to visit the famous Comstock Lode, which was enormously rich. During a brief stopover in Salt Lake City, then with about twenty thousand inhabitants, he complimented the community as being "clean, regularly built, and picturesquely situated," although he disliked the "hideous exterior" of the Tabernacle and had strong reservations about the practice of polygamy, then still legal.

To conclude his American travels, Vivian visited Sacramento, San Francisco, the California gold fields, Yosemite, and some of the big tree country.

Vivian returned to New York for his return voyage to England in January 1878. His farewell statement reads: "My wanderings are ended; and in a few hours more I am amongst familiar sounds and faces in the lobbies, waiting for the first division of the Session [Parliament]. I confess to a very comforting sensation at being once more in old haunts. Greatly as I have enjoyed my run amidst so much that was new and strange, I have returned, if possible, more English than I went out."

34. *The Silverado Squatters*

A romantic attachment first brought Robert Louis Stevenson to America. In France, in 1876, Stevenson met the woman who was to be his future wife. She was Fanny Osbourne, who had left her estranged husband behind in California and had gone to Paris to study painting. She and Stevenson were mutually attracted, spent much time together, and were deeply in love by the time she returned to California in 1878.

Stevenson's relatives and friends disapproved of the romance for two principal reasons: She was ten years older than he and was still legally married. He rejected their advice, however, and left Glasgow on August 7, 1879, aboard the steamer *Dovonia,* paused briefly in New York, and then set off on the eleven-day passage by rail to San Francisco.

Ever the prolific author, Stevenson wrote an account of his Atlantic crossing in *The Amateur Emigrant,* followed by *Across the Plains,* which was completed soon after he reached California as a record of his impressions of that six-thousand-mile journey. Letters written to friends in England during the months that followed reveal that his circumstances were frequently desperate. His family had virtually disowned him, and he was short of funds and seriously ill. Thus, the weeks Stevenson spent in and about Monterey, in San Francisco, and at Fanny Osbourne's cottage in Oakland were an ordeal, but one borne with courage.

During his stay in San Francisco, Stevenson met the famous traveler Charles Warren Stoddard, who had spent thirty-five years exploring and writing about out-of-the-way parts of the world. While a guest in Stoddard's home, Stevenson was presented with a copy of his host's *South Sea Idylls,* two Herman Melville novels of the South Seas, *Typee* and *Omoo,* and shown numerous artifacts gathered during a stay in Tahiti several years earlier. From reading these works and talks with Stoddard, Stevenson determined that some day he, too, would visit the exotic South Sea islands.

Another close friend was the well-known artist, Virgil Williams, then head of the San Francisco School of Design. Toward the middle of May 1880, after Mrs. Osbourne's divorce had been granted, she and Stevenson were married, and Williams found a pleasant and inexpensive cottage for their honeymoon near the northern end of the Napa Valley. The climate there was mild and healthful, exactly what Stevenson required; after a series of illnesses, he had been told by his Oakland physician that he must avoid the fogs and cold winds of the Bay area.

The literary consequence of Stevenson's two-month stay in Napa Valley was *The Silverado Squatters.* The work is a chronicle of what went on in a quiet corner of rural California. Stevenson admired the scenic beauty of "the long green valley," with its groves of oak trees and quiet towns and St. Helena, "the Mont Blanc of the California range"; visited the Petrified Forest; viewed the Bale Mill's "enormous overshot water-wheel"; and sampled the region's delicious wines. As an example of the author's charming style, while standing on his mountain ledge one morning at sunrise and looking down on fog-filled lowlands, he wrote: "Napa Valley was gone; gone were all the lower slopes and woody foot-hills of the range; and in their place, not a thousand feet below, rolled a great level ocean."

The people of the countryside entranced Stevenson even more than the beauties of the region's physical setting. He dwelt at length on such characters as ex-seafarer Charles Evans, pioneer vintners Schram and McEachran, Rufe Hanson and his prattling mate, guests and hangers-on at the Toll House, and others. In particular, he was intrigued by Morris Friedberg Kelmar, an affable and resourceful Russian Jewish shopkeeper, whose hypocrisy and general rascality Stevenson viewed with a kind of amused tolerance.

There are reminders today of Stevenson's stay. The highway along the base of the eastern foothills is officially termed the Silverado Trail. The Silverado Museum at St. Helena displays a comprehensive collection of books, manuscripts, letters, portraits, and other memorabilia relating to Stevenson and his work.

Toward the end of 1880, Stevenson returned to his native Scotland. The rest of his life was a series of wanderings or short stays in America and the islands of the Pacific with his wife, his stepson Lloyd Osbourne, to whom he was deeply attached, and part of the time his mother.

His second extended visit to America came in 1887–88. By then, he had become an author of established reputation, and the Scribner firm contracted with him to write a series of monthly articles for its magazine. Drawn by the bracing climate, Stevenson spent the winter of 1887–88 at Saranac among the Adirondack Mountains of New York State. It was the wild scenery and arctic cold of this region that inspired Stevenson to write *The Master of Ballantrae.* An account of his Saranac period is told in Stephen Chalmers's *The Penny Piper of Saranac.*

The Saranac environment was invigorating for Stevenson, but it did not keep him long. He missed the excitement and mystery of the ocean. Consequently, in the summer of 1888 the Stevenson party crossed the continent to return to California. The yacht *Casco* was chartered at San Francisco (which Stevenson called "the most interesting city in the Union"), and the Stevensons sailed out into the romantic island world of the Pacific. For the next three years they voyaged back and forth between different groups of islands hundreds of miles apart, the Hawaiian group north of the equator and the Society Islands and New Caledonia south of the equator. They narrowly avoided shipwreck on several occasions. The wanderers finally found a permanent home in Samoa, where Stevenson spent the last four years of his life.

After Stevenson's death in 1894, Mrs. Stevenson came back to San Francisco and built a beautiful home at the corner of Lombard and Hyde Streets and a rural lodge among the redwoods of the Coast Range.

Edward A. Freeman, 1823–92

35. *Some Impressions of the United States*

When he visited America in 1882, at age fifty-nine, Edward Freeman examined the nation from various perspectives—historical, economic, social, educational, and political. The following year his detailed observations were published in *Some Impressions of the United States.* Because Freeman's career had been principally devoted to the teaching of history at Oxford University, his point of view was basically that of a historian.

According to Freeman, the first question asked by an American of a visitor from abroad was: "What do you think of our country?" The response, he felt, must be tactful to avoid hurt feelings. Often differences are not significant unless the visitor has given a good deal of thought to his or her answer. "To me," remarked Freeman, "most certainly the United States did not seem a foreign country; it was simply England with a difference." Locality was important: "Rural America differs far more from rural England than urban America differs from urban England. There was nothing strange to me in the general look of the great American cities."

Freeman looked on the United States and England as two English-speaking nations—simply severed branches of the same stock—and the same was true to some extent of other English-speaking nations.

He then proceeded to consider specific differences and similarities between the American and English communities. In language, isolation and separation brought changes in written and spoken words, or caused inhabitants to be more conservative in making linguistic changes from the mother land, such as was the case of old French in Quebec. The same word often came to have different meanings in different settings, giving rise to "Americanisms."

In the field of law, Freeman pointed out the importance of lawyers as a class in America, and found "the proportion of them in the legislative bodies both of the States and of the Union something amazing." Unlike in America, in England the positions of barrister and solicitor are considered separate. In England, too, most barristers are concentrated in London, an arrangement not feasible in the United States because of the size of the country and separation of powers among federal and state courts and constitutions.

Freeman was impressed by the differences between American and English churches resulting from the lack of an established church in the United States and the concept of equality of all Christian religions.

Because of his academic connection in England, the universities and colleges of the United States were a subject of special interest to Freeman. The first thing that struck him was "the amazing number of universities and colleges" compared to Britain. In Ohio alone, there were thirty-two degree-granting institutions, some of which were obviously unqualified. On the other hand, there were institutions of distinction, Harvard, Yale, and Cornell among the universities, and Vassar and Wellesley among the women's colleges.

Freeman's observations on some other aspects of American life were revealing. It was "disappointing" he wrote "in seeing next to nothing of the *fauna* of the country," no opossums or raccoons, but some squirrels, chipmunks, deer, turkeys, and buzzards.

Freeman appears to have been amused by Americans' fondness for titles, even though they had no inherited royalty or nobility and took pride in their democratic heritage. The British visitor in America was surprised at being addressed as "Sir" in private life. Neither did Freeman like such titles as "Doctor" or "Professor" because of his academic connection. In some areas of the United States, men were commonly addressed as "Judge" or "Colonel."

He found no objection to "Governor," but "Major" and "Minister" did not seem fitting. Two other titles in frequent use were "Honorable" and "Esquire," the latter chiefly applied to lawyers. Another American practice odd to the English visitor was to precede the given name of an unmarried woman by the title of "Miss," for example, "Miss Mary."

An important element of civilization that Freeman found missing in the more thickly inhabited parts of America was "the utter absence of decent roads." During his stay in Virginia, he noted that walking, riding, and driving were all done with difficulty. "The lack of good roads is a general feature wherever I have been." The roads and city streets were "often simply a mass of mud."

The relationship between large American cities and the states in which they were located struck Freeman as often irrational. As he could hardly conceive of any city except London being the capital of England, he felt, New York City, rather than Albany, should be the capital of New York State, and there were other anomalous situations around the country.

Freeman reserved his concluding comments for a discussion of American newspapers. He found much to criticize in the popular press, and he doubted that the American people were truly represented by their newspapers. He felt that English papers were less often guilty of silliness and ignorance, were generally free from "vulgar personalities," and nationally rather than locally oriented.

Freeman concluded by expressing great pride in the common heritage of the English and American peoples. To him, "the past history and present condition of the United States are a part of the general history of the Teutonic race and specially of its English branch." Americans, in his view, "still remained in all essential points an English people, more English very often than they themselves know, more English, it may be, sometimes than the kinsfolk whom they left behind in their older home."

36. *American Notes*

The name of Rudyard Kipling is associated with India far more than with America. Nevertheless, at age twenty-four, in 1889, he began to form close connections with the United States.

Immediately after his first arrival, in San Francisco, Kipling undertook an extensive tour of the country. His curiosity led him to experience everything: drinking beer in corner saloons and champagne in swanky club rooms, fishing in mountain streams, admiring vast seas of wheat in the Midwest, watching the operation of grain elevators, wading through the blood of Chicago's slaughter houses, attending church services, trying to touch every type of society and every kind of industry and business. His observations are recorded in *American Notes,* which first appeared in 1891 and was generally suppressed.

From the outset, Kipling's comments about American life and customs are scathing. He came with a grievance—anger over the wholesale pirating of his writings by American publishers. He called San Francisco "a mad city—inhabited for the most part by perfectly insane people, whose women are of a remarkable beauty." He was irked by customs officials, annoying reporters, hearing the English language misspoken, the discourtesy of hotel clerks, omnipresent spittoons and spitting habits, and the presence of card sharps and other bunco artists. While in San Francisco, he encountered two crimes of violence and was shocked by the spirit of lawlessness, the custom of carrying a pistol in the pocket, and the contempt for legal formalities.

Even more critical was his treatment of Chicago, where Kipling condemned the smoke-filled air, the city's preoccupation with money, and its total lack of beauty. He felt that it was filled with an uncouth, money-mad population. He was offended by blatant commercial advertising, and the Chicago newspapers' inaccuracies, bad grammar, slang, and lack of dignity gave him a highly unfavorable impression of midwestern journalism. Equally tasteless in his opinion was a church service where the minister, whose sermon used "imagery borrowed from the auction room," appeared "completely in the confidence of God." Kipling's introduction to "the American Eagle screaming for all it was worth" turned him violently against American politics, although he was equally critical of liberal politics in England.

On the basis of his angry and biased comments, it might be supposed that Kipling disliked America and the Americans. On the contrary, he was amused and fascinated by what he saw and heard, made many friends, and often enjoyed himself immensely. The huge size of everything American impressed him: the great number of hogs and cattle in the Chicago slaughter houses, the vast areas of virgin forests, the teeming rivers and lakes, and the enormous wealth of natural resources. He marveled even more at the wealth of natural beauty and thought that neither pen nor brush could ever adequately portray the splendors of the Yellowstone Gorge and the Grand Canyon. While fishing for salmon, he paid tribute to the primeval wonder of the forests and streams around him.

Kipling was deeply troubled by pollution, waste, and other environmental problems that still beset the country. "The Great American nation," he wrote, "very seldom attempts to put back anything that it has taken from Nature's shelves. It grabs all it can and moves on. But the moving-on is nearly finished and the grabbing must stop."

His comments on Chicago are typical of Kipling's feelings about communities of all sizes. As he traveled through the country from West to East, he often noted that the small towns were dirty, unsightly collections of hovels and larger towns and cities even worse. Describing ugly features of New York City streets, he suggests, "In any other land they would be held to represent slovenliness, sordidness, and want of capacity. Here it is explained, not once but many times, that they show the speed at which the city had grown and the enviable indifference of her citizens to matters of detail."

As to the connecting links between towns and cities, Kipling frequently mentions the poor construction of highways, most of which were nothing except trails. Railroads were worse because of their faulty and careless construction and posed great dangers for travelers.

In short, Kipling concluded that Americans had inherited a wealth of natural beauty and resources, but he was disappointed at the unkempt, unsanitary, and even criminal negligence with which the gift had been treated.

Kipling was not naturally hostile to Americans. He found them raw, lawless, "almost more conceited than the English," and cocksure, "but I love them." Physically, he thought, they were a type to be admired—lean, long-limbed, and bronzed. But he was annoyed by, or critical of, various individual traits. One that continually irked him was American speech, which he felt was remote from the English language. He never failed to marvel at Americans' capacity for liquor. Their eating habits were similarly disagreeable, as he watched them stuff themselves for ten minutes three times a day. Another characteristic Kipling observed was Americans' extreme nervousness and their urge to be busy and to get things done quickly—a trait on which much slipshod work could be blamed. He found town pride and patriotism boring. Public meetings were usually marked by excessive praise of the country, of the government, and of the town where the meeting was being held. Nevertheless, despite their elaborate phraseology and glittering metaphors, Kipling felt that the Americans were genuinely patriotic.

Kipling's observations on American women were generally laudatory. In San Francisco, he declared himself to be in love with eight women at one time. He felt that American girls were the most beautiful in the world. Women ruled their homes, he observed. Unlike their sisters of Europe and Asia, they were independent, socially poised, democratic, clever, and able to speak intelligently. Both American women and men married very young, as a rule before they had a chance to enjoy youth.

Kipling felt more at home as he moved east. The historic associations of Boston caught his fancy, and he enjoyed visits to Lexington and Concord. A climax was a visit to Mark Twain at Elmira, where he and Twain had a long talk about copyright, *Tom Sawyer,* the art of autobiography, and other literary topics. His admiration for a great American genius was obvious.

In January 1892, Kipling married a wealthy New England girl, Caroline Starr Balestier, with whose brother Wolcott he had collaborated in writing *The Naulakha.* The young couple purchased a hillside and built a home in Brattleboro, Vermont, where they lived for the next four years while Kipling was busy writing and publishing. This idyllic life came to a halt when he had legal problems with his brother-in-law, Beatty Balestier, and suddenly decided to return to England.

During his sojourn in Vermont, Kipling wrote *From Sea to Shining Sea,* two novels, and several poems and short stories about American life. The stories dealt with fishermen on the Grand Banks, witchcraft in colonial times, Washington and the Indians, American trains, horses, and other topics more or less related to the United States.

Kipling's last visit to America came in the winter of 1898–99. After an exceedingly rough Atlantic passage, he, his wife, and their three children became seriously ill. All recovered except the oldest daughter, Josephine, who succumbed to a combination of dysentery and whooping cough. Kipling returned to England to live until his death in 1936.

A Kipling critic, W. J. Peddicord, reviewing *American Notes,* maintained that "Of all the prejudiced Englishmen who have from time to time visited America perhaps not one was ever so prejudiced as Rudyard Kipling against her people, her government, her institutions, her customs, manners, and laws, her cities and towns—all things, whether in the sea, the air, or the earth beneath." That statement is extreme, for Kipling found much to admire and praise on the basis of his American experience. Another critic, Howard E. Rawlinson, excused Kipling's sharp words by noting that "His discerning eye and photographic mind, like a camera, took an impression of everything, and when he developed the picture he refused to blot out the unpleasant parts." From many passages in his writings, it is clear that Kipling never lost his faith in the future of the American people.

37. *America the Land of Contrasts: A Briton's View of His American Kin*

James Muirhead was uniquely qualified to write about travel in the United States and in other parts of the world. For more than a quarter of a century, he was in charge of the British editions of Baedeker's handbooks of travel. In writing Baedeker's *Handbook to the United States,* he visited every part of the country. His thorough and penetrating analysis contained in *America the Land of Contrasts* was based on many years of travel and residence. As evidence of the book's popularity, it reached its third edition in 1902, four years after the original edition.

Muirhead's approach to his subject was analytical rather than descriptive, with successive chapters dealing with such topics as American society, American women, American children, sports and amusements, and journalism.

In his introductory comments, Muirhead noted that tourists in the Old World expect to see the Swiss Alps, Italian lakes, Gothic cathedrals and other architectural monuments, and great art museums. The United States, too, can offer much of scenic, artistic, picturesque, and historic interest, but in addition, a person in the right frame of mind will be compensated "in watching the workings of civilization under totally new conditions . . . who can appreciate the growth of general comfort at the expense of taste; who delights in promising experiments in politics, sociology, and education; . . . and is ready to accept novelties on their merits."

He concluded that the wider culture and the more liberal views were often found in American women. Furthermore, he asserted that "the woman of New York and other American cities is often conspicuously superior to her husband in looks, manners, and general intelligence." Muirhead added, "What chiefly strikes the stranger in the American woman is her candour, her frankness, her hail-fellow-well-met-edness, her apparent absence of consciousness of self or of sex, her spontaneity, her vivacity, her fearlessness."

One striking difference between American and English girls that Muirhead pointed out was the latter's preoccupation with catching a husband, a type he called "Girl-Anxious-to-Be-Married" because she had been taught that matrimony was her destiny and should be her chief aim in life. An explanation of the difference in attitude was that American girls had always been accustomed to associating on equal terms with men and regarded them as comrades rather than as possible husbands. "She has so many resources, and is so independent, that marriage does not bound her horizon."

Muirhead praised the social relationship of the sexes in the United States, where men and women have greater opportunity to become better acquainted before marriage, there is a higher percentage of marriage for love, and fewer marriages end in divorce than in Britain, in Muirhead's opinion.

A searching test of the state of civilization in any country, Muirhead maintained, is the position of its women, and in this respect he found that the United States lead the world. Women's legal status was firmly established. All professions were open to them, and their right to follow an independent career was fully recognized. Examples Muirhead cited include teaching, lecturing, journalism, the ministry, medicine, law, and business, and even such occupations as dentists, barbers, and steamboat pilots, as of 1898.

Along with being a "paradise of women," in Muirhead's opinion, America was a "paradise of children." "Nowhere is the child so constantly in evidence; nowhere are his wishes so carefully consulted; nowhere is he allowed to make his mark so strongly on society in general." The product of so much attention was unattractive in Muirhead's judgment: "He interrupts the conversations of his elders, he has a voice in every matter, he eats and drinks what seems good to him, he has no shyness or even modesty." Such behavior made "the stranger long strenuously to spank these budding citizens of a free republic, and to send them to bed *instantly.*" Strangely, however, spoiled children were usually not ruined permanently: "the horrid little minx blossoms out into a charming and womanly girl . . . and the cross little boy becomes a courteous and amiable man."

In a chapter on "international misapprehensions" Muirhead attempted to explain the source of misunderstandings that arise between Americans and the English. He felt that part of the problem was that British ignorance of American affairs was considerably greater than American ignorance of Britain's. Americans, Muirhead wrote, were more articulate than their British cousins; in fact, he accuses Americans of being too voluble and talking too much in contrast to the more reticent and reserved British. Often disagreeable to an American, too, is what Muirhead described as British "brutal frankness, brusqueness, and extreme fondness for calling a spade a spade."

Class distinctions are far sharper in England than in the United States and lead to misunderstandings, Muirhead pointed out. The average middle-class Englishman recognizes that a member of the aristocracy is a superior, which the American sees as a sign of servility. Americans do not recognize anyone as superior. Muirhead's explanation is that "the aristocratic prestige is a growth of centuries" that the English have come to accept as readily as the atmosphere. One point of view is that the aristocracy acts as an incubus on the middle classes of Britain, while the lack of an upper class leaves Americans freer and with fewer constraints.

In writing about American society, Muirhead was concerned not with a fashionable, aristocratic elite such as New York's Four Hundred, but with O. Henry's Four Million. The smaller, self-selected group, he insisted, is "entirely at variance with the spirit of the country and contradictory of its political system." The national trend was toward equality. The good society welcomed to its ranks "everyone of agreeable manners or cultivated mind." A disagreeable aspect of American society, in Muirhead's view, was "its tendency to attach undue importance to materialistic effects." This was shown by "an appallingly vulgar and ostentatious display of mere purchase power. . . . The society of the great mass of Americans shows distinctly more variety than that of England," Muirhead found, in social meetings and in business. "Americans," he said, "are born dancers."

Muirhead devoted little space to American politics. He concluded that political corruption existed more commonly in the United States than in Britain, especially in municipal government. He quoted a cynical statement by a wealthy citizen to the effect that personal interest must be the only possible reason for working and voting for a political party.

All varieties of sports and amusements, American and English, were considered by Muirhead from varying points of view. Despite the tremendous attention to athletics in the United States, he was convinced that the love of sport is more genuine and universal in Britain than in America. In Britain, he felt, there is more general participation in sports and games, less emphasis on winning at all costs, and a less rampant spirit of professionalism. The paraphernalia of sport and strenuous training receive much more attention in the States. A comparison of cricket and baseball brings out differences in national temperments. Cricket is primarily a game for the leisure class, played at a leisurely pace and little touched by professionalism. The best baseball players are highly paid professionals, and a game is usually finished in less than two hours.

As for natural scenery, Muirhead declared that a European would be amply repaid for crossing the Atlantic to see the Yosemite Valley, Yellowstone Park, Niagara, the Grand Canyon, "primeval woods and countless lakes of the Adirondacks," the Hudson (that grander American Rhine), the Swiss-like White Mountains, the Catskills, the mystic Ocklawaha of Florida, and the Black Mountains of Carolina.

Muirhead also analyzed the comparative merits of English and American humor. He observed that the American does not wish a joke underlined, but wants to be tickled by the feeling that a keen eye is required to see the point. An English audience is usually slower than an American one to respond to a joke that is anything less than obvious. Thus, the English are accused of being obtuse and not reacting to subtle humor. The humor of exaggeration is more appreciated by the American, although Muirhead maintained that exaggeration alone is not necessarily funny. Another characteristic of American humor he felt is that it has no reverence for those in position or authority—evidence that Americans do not take themselves too seriously. Summing up, Muirhead commented "we cannot help noticing how humor penetrates and gives savor to the *whole* of American life. . . . The tremendous seriousness with which the Englishman takes himself and everything else is practically unknown in America. . . . Humor acts as a great safety-valve for the excitement of political contests."

Muirhead described American journalism as "a mixed blessing." Like many visitors from abroad, he was highly critical of certain aspects of American newspapers. "The American," he found, "represents a distinctly lower level of life than the English one . . . it caters for the least intelligent class of its readers." The blame for this situation was "the mass of half-educated people in the United States." The American press was credited with being far ahead of old-world newspapers in enterprise shown in the quantity of news collected, but suffered badly in the quality. Worst of all, he felt, were the Sunday editions of the larger papers, "whose endless columns are filled with scandal, politics, crochet-patterns, bogus interviews, puerile hoaxes, highly seasoned police reports, exaggerations of every kind, records of miraculous cures, funny stories with comic cuts, society paragraphs, gossip about foreign royalties, personalities of every description." Muirhead also blamed the press's frequent invasion of privacy.

At the same time, he recognized some important virtues in the American press: "an inspiring sense of largeness and freedom . . . absence of slavish reference to effete authority, the same openness of opportunity, the same freshness of outlook, the same spontaneity of expression, the same readiness in windbag piercing."

Muirhead complemented his discussion of the American press with an analysis of the American and English literary scene, especially a detailed comparison of best-selling books in the two countries. He was high in his praise of the works of Henry James,

W. D. Howells, and Emily Dickinson, and paid tribute to the monthly magazines for their influence in the development of the American short story.

The remainder of *America the Land of Contrasts* is concerned with guide-book information, Muirhead's own principal business. One chapter is entitled "Certain Features of Certain Cities," and another "Baedekeridna" is concerned with railway and steamer travel, hotels, restaurants, postal, and telegraph service.

Muirhead dedicated his book "To the Land that has given me what makes life most worth living."

38. *The Future in America*

H. G. Wells made his first visit to the United States in 1906, as he neared forty years of age. It became clear that he was more interested in the nation's future than in its past. He brought a more individual point of view than British travelers in general. Wells was a Socialist with fairly fixed ideas about requirements for human progress. Like many British intellectuals, his views had been influenced by Henry George's book, *Progress and Poverty,* dealing with the American experience, and he was familiar with the writings of American novelists critical of the American way of life. Another work shown to have inspired Wells's tendency to gaze into the future was Edward Bellamy's *Looking Backward, 2000–1887.*

Wells was a thoroughly friendly critic who trusted in the greatness of the United States, with full confidence in the ability of its people to achieve an even better future. In a chapter of his *The Future in America,* "Growth Invincible," he wrote on a trip from Chicago to Washington as he watched the country fly by, "I got still more clearly the enormous scale of this American destiny." The fundamental character of the nation, as seen by Wells, was gigantic vigor and growth.

At the same time, Wells was deeply disturbed by certain much-publicized events at the time of his visit. Government authorities had just thrown an English labor agitator, William MacQueen, into prison on an unfounded charge that he was an anarchist and had incited a Paterson, New Jersey, mob to a riot. In another case, some newspapers were trying to hound out of the country Maxim Gorky, who was traveling with a fellow Russian, his common-law wife, Maria Andreleva. Wells saw these as instances of American injustice and was highly critical of both.

A social cause about which Wells was most indignant was child labor. The exploitation of children in factories, mines, agriculture, and workshops was a black mark against American society in his opinion, and he cited pathetic examples that he witnessed personally. He blamed the exploitation on a larger evil: American commercial ruthlessness and total preoccupation with money-getting, exemplified by the Standard Oil Company's efforts to crush all competitors. He was alarmed to see enormous aggregations of wealth in the hands of a limited number of individuals and the conspicuous manner in which many of the rich squandered their money.

Wells regarded commercial corruption and political corruption as two sides of the same coin. He saw some advantages in the boss system that prevailed in larger cities, noting that the boss "is very kind to all his crowd. He helps them when they are in trouble, even if it is trouble with the police; he helps them to find employment when they are down on their luck; he stands between them and the impacts of an unsympathetic and altogether too careless social structure in a sturdy and almost parental way."

The great tide of immigrants pouring into the United States from Southern and Eastern Europe posed acute problems for the country, according to Wells. He gives a graphic description of a visit to Ellis Island, during which he saw an endless line, ship load after ship load, of would-be Americans from Ireland, Poland, Italy, Syria, Finland, and Albania. In one month, 21,000 immigrants came into the port of New York alone, and in a year's time there was a total of 1,200,000. As Wells saw it, the horde of newcomers weakened the labor movement, served the purpose of municipal corruption, and complicated social development. The immigrants were wanted by American industry to provide cheap labor, but were converted, declared Wells, "into a practically illiterate industrial proletariat."

A different kind of social problem is the subject of another chapter in *The Future in America,* "The Tragedy of Color." Wells deeply admired the heroism with which thousands of blacks tried to get ahead and improve their lot. Between Booker T. Washington, who was willing to accept the fact of racial separation, and W. E. B. DuBois, who rebelled against the system, he agreed with the latter. In interviews, he found Washington adamant in his views. Wells sought information on the racial situation from all sorts of Americans, but reported that he could not get even "the beginnings of an answer." Furthermore, "hardly any Americans at all seem to be in possession of the elementary facts in relation to this question." Race prejudice was found as "bullying and insolent in the North as in the South."

Wells was most critical of the lawlessness, disorder, and chaos of American life. He constantly emphasized the need for discipline, constructiveness, and purpose. The immense activity that he observed in New York, for example, gave him a feeling of "souless gigantic forces." He felt that Chicago, with the reek and dirt of its stockyards, the endless smoking chimneys and blazing furnaces, the wilderness of grain elevators, factories, and warehouses along the river, the dust and clangor of State Street, was urgently in need of discipline.

Many of Wells's findings on the failures of American society coincided with the conclusions of a number of prominent muckrakers of his time such as Upton Sinclair on the stockyards, Lincoln Steffens on municipal corruption, and Ida Tarbell on the oil corporations. Wells saw their work as evidence that Americans were becoming alert and questioning, aware of the intricate issues of the day—none too soon in his estimation. In later visits he found that the American mind seemed more mature, the nation was becoming conscious of its strength and wished to get rid of its possible weaknesses.

Wells formed a lasting friendship with Theodore Roosevelt, whom he visited several times in the White House. To Wells, Roosevelt was "a very symbol of the creative will in man, in its limitations, its doubtful adequacy, its valiant persistence amid perplexities and confusions. In his undisciplined hastiness, his limitations, his prejudices, his unfairness, his frequent errors, just as much as his force, his sustained courage, his integrity, his open intelligence, he stands for his people and his kind." Any skepticism on Wells's part about the future of America was counterbalanced by Roosevelt's optimism, insisting that even if everything ends in failure "the effort—the effort's worth it."

Other friends included Jane Addams and her staff, whom he visited at Hull House in Chicago to discuss the Fabian Society, the British reformist socialist group of which he was one of the founders.

Wells had intended to visit San Francisco, but the great earthquake and fire in April 1906, while he was in New York forced him to cancel the West Coast tour. He had to be content, therefore, with visiting New York, Boston, Chicago, and Washington.

Despite his reservations about the United States, as expressed in *The Future in America,* Wells was convinced of what he called "the birth strength of a splendid civilization." He added:

> I see it, the vast rich various continent, the gigantic energetic process of development, the acquisitive successes, the striving failures, the multitudes of those rising and falling who come between, all set in a texture of spacious countryside, animate with pleasant timber homes, of clangorous towns that bristle to the skies, of great exploitation districts and crowded factories, of wide deserts and mine-torn towns, and huge half-tamed rivers.

Henry James, a close friend, wrote to Wells in criticism of *The Future in America* that the book was "too *loud,* as if the country shouted at you, hurrying fast, every hint it has to give and you yelled back your comment on it; but also, frankly I think the right and only way to utter many of the things you are delivered of is to yell them—it's a yelling country, and the voice must pierce or dominate."

Wells made repeated visits to the United States for short periods in 1921, 1934, 1935, 1937, and 1940. He hoped that the nation would take the lead in creating an international government. He never lost interest in America or ceased to question its destiny. In 1928, he wrote, "America is part of my spiritual home and Old Glory one of my quarterings. I have a loyal feeling for the American eagle."

39. *Good-bye, America!*

No journalist of his time had a more active career than Henry W. Nevinson. As a war correspondent, he was involved in every military conflict of importance starting with the Greco-Turkish conflict of 1897. He was in Spain during the Spanish-American War; in South Africa throughout the Boer War; in Russia during the revolutionary uprising of 1905; in the Balkans during the fighting there in 1911–13; and he saw action on many fronts in World War I. In addition, he visited Central Africa in 1904–5 and exposed the Portuguese slave trade in Angola and elsewhere. He was associated with the *Daily Chronicle* (1897–1903), the *London Nation* (1906–23), *Daily News* (1908–9), and was correspondent for the *Manchester Guardian* in the attack on the Dardanelles and later in Salonika and Egypt during World War I.

The following article appeared in the *London Nation* and was later reprinted in book form in 1922 in *Good-bye, America!*, when the author arrived home from a visit to the Washington Peace Conference.

> In mist and driving snow the towers of New York fade from view. The great ship slides down the river. Already the dark, broad seas gloom before her. Good-bye, most beautiful of modern cities! Good-bye to glimmering spires and lighted bastions, dreamlike as the castles and cathedrals of a romantic vision! Good-bye to thin films of white steam that issue from central furnaces and flit in dissolving wreaths around those precipitous heights!
>
> Good-bye to the copious meals—early grapefruit, the 'cereals,' eggs broken in a glass! Good-bye to oysters, large and small, to celery and olives beside the soup, to 'sea food,' to sublimated viands, to bleeding duck, to the salad course, to the 'individual pie' or the thick wedge of

apple pie, to the invariable slab of ice cream, to the coffee, also bland with cream; to the home-brewed alcohol! I am going to the land of joints and roots and solid pudding; the land of ham and eggs and violent tea; the land where oysters are good for suicides alone, and where mustard grows and whiskey flows. Good-bye, America! I am going home.

Good-bye to the long stream of motors—'limousines' or 'flivvers'! Good-bye to the signal lights upon Fifth Avenue, gold, crimson, and green; the sudden halt when the green light shines, as though at the magic word an enchanted princess had fallen asleep; the hurried rush for the leisurely lunch at noon; the deliberate appearance of hustle and bustle in business; the Jews, innumerable as the Red Sea sand! Good-bye to outside staircases for escape from fire. Good-bye to scrappy suburbs littered with rubbish of old boards, empty cans, and boots! Good-bye to standardized villages and small towns alike in litter, in ropes of electric wires along the streets, in clanking 'trolleys' in chapels, stores, railway stations, Main Streets, and isolated houses flung at random over the country! Good-bye to miles of advertisement imploring me in ten-foot letters to eat somebody's codfish ('No Bones!') or smoke somebody's cigarettes ('They Satisfy'), or sleep with innocence in the "Faultless Nightgown"! Good-bye to long trains where one smokes in a lavatory, and sleeps at night upon a shelf screened with heavy green curtains and heated with stifling air, while over your head or under your back the baby yells, and the mother tosses moaning, until at last you reach your 'stopping-off place,' and a semi-Negro sweeps you down with a little broom, as in a supreme rite of worship! Good-bye to the house that is labeled 'One Hundred Years Old,' for the amazement of mortality! Good-bye to thin woods and fields inclosed with casual pales, old hoops and lengths of wire! I am going to the land of a policeman's finger, where the horse and the bicycle still drag out a lingering life; a land of old villages and towns as little like each other as one woman is like the next; a land where trains are short, and one seldom sleeps in them, for in any direction within a day they will reach a sea; a land of vast and ancient trees, of houses time-honored three centuries ago, of cathedrals that have been growing for a thousand years, and of village churches built while people believed in God. Good-bye, America! I am going home.

Good-bye to the land of a new language in growth, of split infinitives and cross-bred words; the land where a dinner jacket is a 'Tuxedo,' a spittoon a 'cuspidor'; where your opinion is called your 'reaction,' and where 'vamp,' instead of meaning an improvised accompaniment to song, means a dangerous female! Good-bye to the land where grotesque exaggeration is called humor, and people gape in bewilderment at irony, as a bullock gazes at a dog straying in his field! Good-bye to the land where strangers say, 'Glad to meet you, sir,' and really seem glad; where children whine their little desires, and never grow much older; where men keep their trousers up with belts that run through loops, and women have to bathe in stockings! I am going to a land of ancient speech where we still say 'record' and 'concord' for 'recud' and 'concud,' where 'necessarily' and 'extraordinarily' must be taken at one rush—a hedge-ditch-and-rail in the hunting field; where we do not 'commute' or 'check' or 'page,' but 'take a season' and 'register' and 'send a boy round'; where we never say we are glad to meet a stranger, and seldom are; where humor is understatement and irony is our habitual resource in danger or distress; where children are told they are meant to be seen and not heard; where it is 'bad form' to express emotions, and suspenders are a strictly feminine article of attire. Good-bye, America! I am going home.

Good-bye to the multitudinous papers, indefinite of opinion, crammed with insignificant news, and asking you to continue a first-page article on page 23, column 5! Good-bye to the weary platitude, accepted as wisdom's latest revelation! Good-bye to the docile audiences that lap rhetoric for substance! Good-bye to politicians contending for aims more practical than principles! Good-bye to Republicans and Democrats, distinguishable only by mutual hatred! Good-bye to the land where Liberals are thought dangerous and Radicals show red! Where Mr. Gompers is called a Socialist, and Mr. Asquith would seem advanced! A land too large for concentrated indignation; a land where wealth beyond the dreams of British profiteers dwells, dresses, gorges, and luxuriates, emulated and unashamed! I am going to a land of politics violently divergent; a land where even coalitions cannot coalesce; where meetings break up in a turbulent disorder, and no platitude avails to soothe the savage beast; a land fierce for personal freedom and indignant with rage for justice; a land where wealth is taxed out of sight, or for very shame strives to disguise its luxury; a land where an ancient order is passing away and leaders whom you call extreme are hailed by Lord Chancellors as the very fortifications of security. Good-bye, America! I am going home.

Good-bye to prose chopped up to look like verse! Good-bye to the indiscriminate appetite, which gulps lectures as opiates and 'printed matter' as literature! Good-bye to the wizards and witches who ask to psychoanalyze my complexes, inhibitions, and silly dreams! Good-bye to the exuberant religious or fantastic beliefs by which unsatisfied mankind still strives desperately to penetrate beyond the flaming bulwarks of the world! Good-bye, Americans! I am going to a land very much like yours. I am going to your spiritual home.

40. *The American Character*

A logical successor to Alexis de Tocqueville and James Bryce as a student of American history and politics was Denis W. Brogan, professor of political science at the University of Cambridge. His fascination with the United States began early. In 1933, he published *The American Political System,* hailed by critics as qualified to stand beside Bryce's *American Commonwealth* for its remarkable understanding. Brogan was a frequent visitor to the United States, and during World War II he directed the American division of the British Broadcasting Company. Henry Steele Commager maintained that "no other Britisher of our time has brought to an understanding of the American character and institutions a more intimate familiarity with or a warmer affection for this country." These qualities are clearly evident throughout Brogan's brilliant work, *The American Character,* published in 1944.

At the outset, Brogan stated, "My object has been to make what I think is the most interesting country interesting and intelligible to others." In his view, "there is no parallel in history to the experiment of free government on this scale."

Approximately one-half of *The American Character* is concerned with the subject "America Is Made." What were the forces that transformed a huge wilderness into present-day America? Brogan recounted the long and difficult historical process. Tens of millions of Europeans crossed the Atlantic to begin new lives. The first settlers were confronted by a million square miles of primeval forest from Maine to Florida. Several hundred thousand Indians, mainly hostile, roamed over a vast continent. The new settlers had to devise different agricultural methods to deal with conditions unfamiliar to them, as well as problems of climate. American political and social systems gradually replaced European importations. The evolution of these complex factors over a period of nearly five hundred years is brilliantly analyzed by Brogan in *The American Character.*

In the early years, colonists along the East Coast maintained fairly close contact with the mother country. As settlers moved inland, however, they ran a formidable risk of war with the Iroquois and other Indian tribes, a fact that slowed westward advance for at least a generation. Great courage was required of the eighteenth-century settlers who crossed the mountain barrier and entered the Mississippi Valley. Nevertheless, they came year after year by tens of thousands, crowded out the Indians, established towns and cities, and in many cases cleared the land to become farmers.

It was an extremely hard world for women, and the death rate was high among them and their children. Brogan discussed women's efforts to bring stability and some degree of civilization to frontier life, aided by such political leaders as Andrew Jackson, Henry Clay, and Sam Houston. The pioneers set up effective local government suited to their needs.

Two American wars, the Revolution, and especially the Civil War, made permanent impacts on the American mind. It had taken 250 years for the English-speaking settlers to move from the Atlantic to the Missouri River, but within five years after the end of the Civil War, the final 1,500 miles to California had been bridged, although there were settlers in California before the war. A tremendous boost came with completion of transcontinental railroads. Brogan called the great western movement "one of the most decisive campaigns in world history; won in nearly three hundred years of ceaseless battle."

Marring this optimistic outlook were special problems faced in several regions of the country. In the South and Mississippi Valley, the settlers had to deal with such diseases as yellow fever, pellagra, hookworm, and malaria. The South was handicapped climatically, historically, racially, and economically. Even California, with its nearly perfect climate, had earthquakes, floods, fire, fog and smog, while the "rival paradise of Florida" had killing frosts, tornados, and hurricanes. "In other parts of America," as Brogan pointed out, "the savage possibilities of the climate are never forgotten," both in winter and summer.

Brogan saw women as the beneficiaries of increased American wealth, as the income of most families made more comfortable lives possible. Specifically, he mentioned the sewing machine, effective home heating, good oil lamps, running water, the development of anesthetics, washing machines, the telephone, gas stoves, electric ranges, and efficient can-openers—as all making life easier for women. By the second half of the nineteenth century, women were becoming the leaders of various reform movements: prohibition, banning organized prostitution, and agitation in support of world peace.

Brogan emphasized the key role of the farmer in American history: "The conquest of the United States by plow, has been the most generally approved American victory." At the same time, the farmer had experienced numerous ups and downs. Farming is a gamble, affected by economic depressions, crop failures, weather, insects, and fluctuating prices. As a consequence, farmers have had to make constant readjustments, causing unhappiness and resentment against forces over which they have no control.

Problems of government for a nation of more than three million square miles have been successfully resolved in the United States, in Brogan's view: "To have created a free government, over a continental area, without making a sacrifice of adequate efficiency or of liberty is the American achievement. It is a unique achievement in world history."

The foregoing are among the important aspects Brogan saw as shaping the history of the American people from the earliest days to the twentieth century. In Part 2, "Unity and Liberty," he examined the diverse racial mixture of the American population, the early role of religion in unifying the country, conflicts between Catholics and Protestants, the abiding influence of the Civil War on southern mores, and the rising impact of special interests on American politics.

Near the end of *The American Character,* Brogan tackled the subject of American schools from kindergarten to universities. He found that the term "school" applied to every type of educational institution at all levels. Schools' prime purpose, to instruct the students "in how to live in America," is complicated by the diversity of the student population. Many are children of immigrants to whom English is a foreign language; another large proportion is children of migrants from different parts of the United States; and Central or South America; others are children of rural-bred parents adjusting to an urban world new to them. The schools have the responsibility for teaching them a common language, common habits, and a common political and national faith. "In many cases," Brogan asserted, "the colleges are doing what is really high school work." The schools' political function is to teach Americanism, that is, political and patriotic dogma and habits necessary to American life. Reverence for the flag in an American school is often analogous to a religious ritual.

Brogan saw the diversity of curricula and school activities as justified on such grounds as students learning about American ways of life, practical politics, organization, and social ease. Reminiscent of Noah Webster is his discussion of the emergence of an American language distinctive in many ways from standard English. He called the creation of general literacy and a common written and spoken tongue a remarkable American achievement.

The importance that sports play in the advancement of under-privileged students is pointed out by Brogan. Because sport is democratic, blacks and children of immigrants can quickly win prestige and recognition through their ability.

Brogan complimented the "first-class academic work" done in American universities, such as reinterpretations of American history and the study of world affairs. Not only in universities, but also in leading newspapers and magazines, in forums, and on the air is serious discussion of such matters "incessant."

In *The American Character,* Brogan's design, he states, is to make certain American principles and attitudes more intelligible to the British public. He concedes that he treats many important aspects of American life sketchily, or ignores them entirely. Nevertheless, he produced a remarkably perceptive and penetrating study of American history and society. In the end, he urged that Americans recognize the position of the United States as a world power and the need for a new world society. Near the end of World War II he wrote that "The house must cease to be divided if we are to prevent one of the ice ages of history from coming upon us."

Bibliography

Arnold, Matthew (1822–88)

> *Civilization in the United States* (Boston, 1888). Later editions: Boston, 1889, 1900; Freeport, N.Y., 1972.
> *References:* Trilling, Lionel, *Matthew Arnold* (New York, 1939) and *The Portable Matthew Arnold* (New York, 1949).

Bishop, Isabella Bird (1831–1904)

> *A Lady's Life in the Rocky Mountains* (New York, 1879–80). First published serially as "Letters from the Rocky Mountains" in *Leisure Hour,* 1878. Appeared in book form under title *A Lady's Life in the Rocky Mountains.* Later editions: London, 1880, 1894, 1900, 1910; New York, 1881, 1882, 1883, 1886, 1887, 1888, 1890, 1893. *References:* Berger, Max, *The British Traveller in America* (New York, 1943); Boorstein, Daniel, "Introduction" to *A Lady's Life in the Rocky Mountains* (Norman, Okla., 1960); Stoddart, Anna M., *The Life of Isabella Bird (Mrs. Bishop)* (London, 1907).

Bremer, Frederika (1801–65)

> *The Homes of the New World: Impressions of America* (London and New York, 1853). Later editions: New York, 1854, 1864, 1868, 1968. *Reference:* Routh, Signe Alice, *Scenes of the Northland Frederika Bremer: American Journey, 1849–1851* (Philadelphia, 1855).

Brogan, Denis W. (1900–74)

> *The American Character* (New York, 1944). Later edition: New York, 1950. *References:* Brogan, Denis W., *America in the Modern World* (New Brunswick, N.J., 1960); Commager, Henry Steele, *America in Perspective* (New York, 1947).

Bryce, James (1838–1922)

> *The American Commonwealth,* 2 vols. (New York, 1888). Numerous later editions including New York, 1931, 1938, 1941, 1978. *References:* Fisher, Herbert, *James Bryce* (Westport, Conn., 1973); Ions, Edmund S., *James Bryce and American Democracy* (London, 1968).

Buckingham, James Silk (1786–1855)

> *The Eastern and Western States of America,* 3 vols. (London, 1842).

References: Buckingham, James Silk, *Autobiography,* 2 vols. (London, 1855); Nevins, Allan, *America Through British Eyes* (New York, 1948); Turner, Ralph E., *James Silk Buckingham* (London, 1934).

Burton, Richard Francis (1821–90)

The City of the Saints and Across the Rocky Mountains to California (London, 1861). Later editions: London and New York, 1862. *References:* Brodie, Fawn, *The Devil Drives* (New York, 1967); Burton, Isabel, *Life of Richard Francis Burton* (London, 1893); Dodge, W. P., *The Real Sir Richard Burton,* (London, 1907); Nevins, Allan, *America Through British Eyes* (New York, 1948); Richard, A. B. et al., *A Sketch of the Career of Richard Francis Burton* (London, 1886); Stisted, G. M., *The True Life of Captain Sir Francis Burton* (London, 1896); Wright, Thomas, *A Life* (London, 1960).

Chastellux, Francois Jean, Marquis de (1734–88)

Travels in North America in the Years 1780, 1781, and 1782. Later editions: Paris, 1786, 1788–91; Dublin and London, 1787; New York, 1827, 1828; Chapel Hill, N.C., 1963, 2 vols. *Reference:* Unwin, Kenneth, *Georges Chastellux* (Paris, 1937).

Cobbett, William (1783–1835)

A Year's Residence in the United States of America, 3 vols. (Boston, 1818). Later editions: London, 1819, 1822, 1828; Belfast, 1818; Carbondale, Ill., 1964. *References:* Chesterton, G. K., *Life of William Cobbett* (London, 1925); Clark, Mary Elizabeth, *Peter Porcupine in America: The Career of William Cobbett, 1792–1800* (Gettysburg, Pa., 1939); Cole, G. D. H., *Life of William Cobbett,* 3rd. ed. (London, 1947); Gaines, Pierre W., *William Cobbett and the United States* (Worcester, Mass., 1975).

Crowe, Eyre (1824–1910)

With Thackeray in America (London and New York, 1893).

Dicey, Edward (1832–1911)

Six Months in the Federal States, 2 vols. (London and Cambridge, 1863). *References:* Dicey, Edward, *Spectator of America* (Chicago, 1971); Nevins, Allan, *America Through British Eyes* (New York, 1948).

Dickens, Charles (1812–70)

American Notes (London, 1842). Numerous later editions. *References:* Butt, John, *Dickens at Work* (London, 1958); Ford, G. H., *Dickens and His Makers* (Princeton, N.J.: 1955); Forster, John, *Life of Charles Dickens* (London, 1822–74); House, A. H., *The Dickens World* (London, 1941); Johnson, Edgar, *Charles Dickens, His Tragedy and Triumph* (New York, 1952); Nevins, Allan, *America Through British Eyes* (New York, 1948).

Freeman, Edward A. (1823–92)

Some Impressions of the United States (London and New York, 1883).

Reference: Stevens, W. R. W., *The Life and Letters of Edward A. Freeman* (London, 1895).

Fukuzawa, Yukichi (1824–1901)
Autobiography, trans. Eichi Kiyooka (Tokyo, 1934, 1940, 1947, 1948). *Reference:* Miyamori, Asataro, *A Life of Mr. Yukichi Fukuzawa* (Tokyo, 1902).

Hall, Basil (1788–1844)
Travels in North America in the Years 1827 and 1828, 3 vols. (Edinburgh and London, 1827). Later editions: Philadelphia, 1829; London, 1830. *References:* Biddle, Richard, *Captain Hall in America* (Philadelphia, 1830); Colton, Calvin, *The Americans* (London, 1833); Nevins, Allan, *America Through British Eyes* (New York, 1948).

Kalm, Peter (1716–79)
Travels into North America, 1753–61 (London, 1770 and 1772). Later edition: Barre, Mass., 1972. *References:* Kalm, Peter, *The America of 1750* (New York, 1937); Kerkkomen, Marti, *Peter Kalm's North American Journey* (Helsinki, 1959); Olsson, Nils William, *Peter Kalm and the Image of North America* (Minneapolis, 1970).

Kemble, Frances Ann (Fanny) (1809–93)
Journal of a Residence on a Georgia Plantation in 1838–1839 (New York, 1863). Later editions: London, 1863; New York, 1864; Athens, Ga., 1984. *Records of a Later Life* (London, 1882); *Journal of a Residence in America* (London, 1835). *References:* Armstrong, Margaret, *Fanny Kemble* (New York, 1938); Bobbé, Dorothie, *Fanny Kemble* (New York, 1931); Driver, Leota, *Fanny Kemble* (Chapel Hill, N.C.: 1933); Marshall, Dorothy, *Fanny Kemble* (New York, 1977): Rushmore, Robert, *Fanny Kemble* (New York, 1970).

Kipling, Rudyard (1865–1936)
American Notes (Boston, 1899). Other editions: New York, 1889, 1891, 1893, 1894, 1896, 1899; Philadelphia, 1899; Norman, Okla., 1981. *References:* Carrington, C. E., *Life and Work of Rudyard Kipling* (Garden City, N.Y., 1955); Hopkins, R. T., *Rudyard Kipling* (London, 1921); Peddicord, W. J., *Kipling Revisited* (Portland, 1980); Rawlinson, Howard E., *View of the American Scene and Character* (Urbana, Ill., 1938); Tompkin, J. M. S., *The Art of Rudyard Kipling* (London, 1959).

Lakier, Aleksandr Borisovich (1825–70)
A Russian Looks at America . . . The Journey in 1857 (Chicago, 1879). *Reference:* Bliven, Naomi, *The New Yorker* 55 (Feb. 4, 1980): 117–20.

Lyell, Charles (1797–1875)
Travels in North America (London, 1845–49). Later editions: New York, 1845, 1852, 1856; London, 1855; Salem, N. H., 1978. *A Second Visit to the United States of North America,* 2 vols. (London, 1849). *References:* Bailey, Edward B., *Charles Lyell* (Garden City, N.Y., 1963);

Bonney, Thomas G., *Charles Lyell and Modern Geology* (New York, 1895); Commager, Henry Steele, *America in Perspective* (New York, 1947); Wilson, Leonard G., *Charles Lyell* (New Haven, 1922). *Life, Letters and Journals of Sir Charles Lyell,* 2 vols. (London, 1881).

Mackay, Alexander (1808–52)
The Western World, 2 vols. (Philadelphia, 1819). Later editions: London, 1849, 1850; Philadelphia, 1849; New York, 1968.

Macrae, David (1837–1907)
The Americans at Home, 2 vols. (Edinburgh, 1870). Later editions: Glasgow, 1874, 1875, 1886, 1908; New York, 1952. *America Revisited* (Glasgow, 1908).

Marryat, Frederick (1792–1848)
A Diary in America, 3 vols. (London, 1839). Later editions: London, 1842; New York, 1839; Philadelphia, 1840; Paris, 1839, 1840; Westport, Conn., 1973. *References:* Gautier, Maurice Paul, *Captain Frederick Marryat* (Montreal, 1973); Hannay, David, *Life of Frederick Marryat* (London, 1889); Strong, George Templeton, *Diary* (New York, 1952); Warner, Oliver, *Captain Marryat, a Rediscovery* (London, 1953).

Martineau, Harriet (1802–76)
A Retrospect of Western Travel, 3 vols. (London, 1838). Later editions: Cincinnati, 1838; New York, 1838; Westport, Conn., 1969. *References:* Colson, Percy, *Victorian Portraits* (Freeport, N.Y., 1968); Nyvill, John C., *Harriet Martineau* (London, 1944); Webb, Robert K., *Harriet Martineau* (London, 1960).

Michaux, Francois André (1770–1855)
Travels to the West of the Allegheny Mountains into Ohio, Kentucky, and Tennessee (London, 1805; Cleveland, 1904). *Reference:* Michaux, F. A., *The North American Silva,* 5 vols. (Philadelphia, 1857).

Muirhead, James F. (1853–1934)
America, the Land of Contrasts: A Briton's View of His American Kin (London, 1898). Later editions: London and New York, 1902, 1911, 1970. *Reference:* Baedeker, Karl, *The United States* (Leipzig, 1909), prepared by James F. Muirhead.

Nevinson, Henry (1856–1941)
Good-Bye, America! (New York, 1922), reprint: *Farewell to America* (New York, 1973). *References:* Commager, Henry Steele, *America in Perspective* (New York, 1947); Nevinson, Henry, *Visions and Memories* (London, 1946).

Nuttall, Thomas (1786–1859)
A Journal of Travels into the Arkansas Territory during the Year 1819 (Philadelphia, 1821; Norman, Okla., 1980). References: *Dictionary of National Biography,* vol. 14, pp. 721–22; Graustein, Jeannette, E., *Thomas Nuttall, Naturalist, Exploration in America,* 1808–1841 (Cambridge, Mass., 1967); Morrison, Samuel Eliot, *Three Centuries of Harvard*

(Cambridge, Mass., 1936); Nuttall, Thomas, *A Popular Handbook of the Ornithology of the United States and Canada* (Boston, 1891), *Collections towards Three Flora of the Territory of Arkansas* (1834), and *Travels into the Old Northwest* (Waltham, Mass., 1951).

Oliver, William (n.d.)
Eight Months in Illinois (Newcastle, 1843). Later edition: Chicago, 1924. *Reference:* Berger, Max, *The British Traveler in America* (New York, 1943).

Russell, William H. (1820–1907)
My Diary North and South (Boston, 1863). Later editions: London, 1863; New York, 1864; Norwood, Pa., 1977. *References:* Atkins, John Black, *The Life of Sir William Howard Russell* (London, 1911); Furneaux, Robert, *The First War Correspondent: William Howard Russell of the Times* (London, 1945); Nevins, Allan, *America Through British Eyes* (New York, 1943).

Sarmiento, Domingo Faustino (1811–88)
Travels in the United States in 1847 (Princeton, N.J., 1890, 1970). *References:* Bunkley, Allison W., *The Life of Sarmiento* (Princeton, N.J., 1952); Correas, Edmundo, *Sarmiento and the United States* (Gainesville, Fla., 1961); Crowley, Frances G. *Domingo Faustino Sarmiento* (New York, 1977).

Somers, Robert (1822–91)
The Southern States since the War (London and New York, 1871, 1893). *Reference:* Nevins, Allan, *America Through British Eyes* (New York, 1943).

Stevenson, Robert Louis (1850–94)
The Silverado Squatters (London, 1883). Numerous editions: 1884–1923; Ashland, Ore., 1972. *References:* Chesterton, G. K., *Robert Louis Stevenson* (London, 1955); Issler, Anne R., *Stevenson at Silverado* (San Francisco, 1939) and *Happier for His Presence* (San Francisco, 1949); Pearce, Catherine O. *Robert Louis Stevenson* (1955).

Stuart-Wortley, Lady Emmeline (1806–55)
Travels in the United States, etc. during 1849 and *1850* (New York, 1851). Later editions: London, 1851; New York, 1868. *References:* Cust, Nina, *Wanderers: Episodes from the Travels of Lady Emmeline Stuart-Wortley and Her Daughter Victoria, 1849–1855* (New York, 1928.)

Tocqueville, Alexis de (1805–59)
Democracy in America (Paris, 1835). Numerous editions: London, Paris, New York, Cambridge; best modern edition: New York, 1945, 2 vols. *References:* Mayer, T. P., *Alexis de Tocqueville* (New York, 1940), Pierson, G. W., *Tocqueville and Beaumont in America* (New York, 1939); Toqueville, Alexis de, *Journey to America,* trans. George Lawrence (New Haven, Conn., 1960).

Trollope, Anthony (1815–82)
North America (London, 1862). Later editions: Leipzig, London, and

New York, 1862; Philadelphia and New York, 1863. *References:* Booth, Bradford A., *Anthony Trollope* (Bloomington, Ind., 1958); Briggs, Asa, *Victorian People* (New York, 1955); Cockshut, Anthony O. J., *Anthony Trollope* (London, 1956); Escott, T. H. S., *Anthony Trollope* (London, 1913); Nevins, Allan, *America Through British Eyes* (New York, 1948).

Trollope, Frances (1780–1865)

The Domestic Manners of the Americans, 2 vols. (London, 1832). Later editions: London, New York, Paris, 1862–1949. *References:* Bigland, Eileen, *The Indomitable Mrs. Trollope* (London, 1953); Brooks, John Graham, *As Others See Us* (New York, 1908); Frasee, Monique, *Mrs. Trollope and America* (Caen, France, 1969); McDermott, John Francis, *A Note on Mrs. Trollope* (Columbus, Ohio, 1936).

Vivian, Arthur Pendarres (1834–1926)

Wanderings in the Western Land (London, 1879 and 1880).

Wansey, Henry (1752–1827)

An Excursion to the United States of North America in the Summer of 1794 (Salisbury, 1796 and 1798; New York, 1969). *References:* Jeremy, David J., *Henry Wansey and His American Journal, 1794* (Philadelphia, 1970); *Dictionary of National Biography,* vol. 20, p. 748.

Wells, Henry George (1866–1946)

The Future of America (New York, 1906). Later editions: Leipzig, 1907; Salem, N.H., 1974. *References:* Belgion, Montgomery, *H. G. Wells* (London, 1953); Beresford, John D., *H. G. Wells* (London, 1972); Brome, Vincent, *H. G. Wells* (London, 1951); Costa, Richard H., *H. G. Wells* (New York, 1967).

Index

227

ROBERT B. DOWNS, library administrative dean, emeritus, University of Illinois, is a distinguished librarian, author, and scholar. To his earned academic degrees in History and Library Science, he has been given six honorary doctorates from colleges and universities in New England, the South, and the Midwest. Mr. Downs has received the Clarence Day and the Joseph Lippincott Awards for his written works in reference librarianship, and the Melvil Dewey Medal for creative, professional achievements of high order. He was also awarded a Guggenheim fellowship for his *British Library Resources,* A. L. A., 1973.

Mr. Downs has received also special citations and honors from the Japanese government for his contributions to the creation of the National Diet Library at Tokyo. Mexico, Turkey, and Afghanistan also received his professional aid. He was chief librarian at Colby College, the University of North Carolina, and New York University before going to Illinois. Mr. Downs served as president of the Illinois Library Association, the Association of College and Research Libraries, and the American Library Association.

Dean Downs is a prolific author; his international bestseller, *Books That Changed the World,* was published in 1956 and remains the centerpiece of his many publications.